China:
The Hidden Miracle

The extraordinary tale of two ordinary people

by

Ross Paterson and Elisabeth Farrell

Foreword by Brother Andrew

Sovereign World

Sovereign World Ltd
PO Box 777
Tonbridge
Kent TN11 9XT
England

ISBN: 1 85240 130 3

Typeset by CRB (Drayton) Typesetting Services, Drayton, Norwich
Printed in England by Clays Ltd, St Ives plc.

To Ye Enshi and Huiliang
and to our brothers and sisters in China
many of whom could tell similar stories.
We look forward to rejoicing with you
on that coming day when every tear is wiped away.

To Christine Paterson,
who gave Ross and Elisabeth so much help.

To Christine Hobson,
and all the other CCSM and DPM-China staff,
who did the 'hidden' work to bring this
'hidden miracle' to light.

Contents

Foreword

There is something in the air today that makes one look at China more closely.

OK, let me start at the beginning. When did it all begin? It was when I was a student at the WEC missionary training college in Glasgow. One afternoon I spent time in the manse of a local minister, enjoying his company and watching television. It seems ages ago now, but I remember it was at a time when there was such famine in China that the people were eating bark right off the trees for want of any other food. And there in public I cried. I cried uncontrollably. I cried like a child. Yet I never quite understood what made me cry. I had seen need before, I had experienced wars, I had seen hunger and I had seen death. But here was something that shook me to the very core of my being. Much, much later I understood that when God gives us a burden for a nation or country, He causes us to weep when we intercede for that place. I personally believe that is a precondition, but I am not dogmatic about it.

Only a few years later, during the infamous Chinese campaign 'We must overtake Britain', I was watching television in the home of one of my friends in Gravesend, Kent. My family were with me, and my wife and I saw the people in China building little ovens to produce steel. Again I cried. There was something in the air that was preparing me for involvement.

Later still, during 1964, just prior to the Cultural Revolution, I was walking on the Great Wall north of Beijing.

There was no one to take a photo of me, but I was there praying for open doors, praying for a miracle, praying that somehow there would be ways and means of getting the Scriptures into China.

Not long after that, I met Ross Paterson. He made a great impression on me. As a matter of fact, I remember one day writing about Ross in our Open Doors circular and calling him 'one of our workers'. Then I suddenly realised that he didn't officially work for us, so I wrote him a letter of apology. He gracefully replied that he thought it was an honour to be called an 'Open Doors worker'. You see, by that time, there was a shared burden among many of God's people around the world. And that is how and when things began to move. Somehow this is God's economy, but don't ask me to explain it.

After that things began to develop. The Cultural Revolution caused untold suffering. It will never be told, but there is One Who keeps records and preserves all the tears in a bottle. It must be a very big bottle for China. But what you ultimately receive is in harmony with the price you paid for it.

Now something is happening in China again. Something I cannot explain, but God is speaking to many people about China. In the mean time the most marvellous changes have taken place in that gigantic country. The Spirit is working in a way that we have probably never seen before in the history of the Church. He has shaken China and brought forth millions who truly believe in Jesus Christ in spite of the lack of teaching and Scriptures. God has enabled us to take millions of Scriptures in. They are much needed and there has never been enough. We have done some teaching, but again it has never been enough. Yet I feel that something is happening.

There are wonderful examples of what God can do. We never doubted it, of course. Yet we never expected the collapse of communism to come in such a dramatic way. We never expected that Albania, the most closed country in the communist block, would open up. We certainly never expected to see over forty evangelical churches spring up within two years in that tiny country where, previously, we had not heard of even one national believer and had not known of even one church. But God was speaking to us.

Today – as I see it – there are two main areas of focus in God's economy: the Middle East and China. But I daresay China is first. God is going to do something and this hidden miracle is still taking place every day in China. It is going to be very open, very obvious, very visible. And all the things that God is preparing now inside China and in the hearts of those concerned, like Ross and his mission, and in my own heart and our Open Doors mission and many others, will one day have such an impact, because we are there. We're writing, we're speaking, we're going inside, teaching, taking in Scriptures, distributing them and simply not accepting that the largest nation in the world is cut off from the open preaching of the Gospel. We believe God has the last word and soon we are going to hear it on China.

That makes it so exciting for me to write these few words as a foreword to Ross Paterson and Elisabeth Farrell's book: *China: The Hidden Miracle*.

Brother Andrew

Preface

The hidden miracle in China is the loving activity of God in a huge and complex nation, activity that has birthed and sustained the fastest growing church of our generation. The Chinese church could have been destroyed by the hand of those who chose to hate it over the last forty and more years. Instead, through the blood and tears, it has grown and flourished – and still does today.

One approach to this miracle would be to seek to catalogue the events that have led to this extraordinary growth. Another approach would be to select a couple whose story, although it is only one story, still represents to us the depth and scope of the miracle that God has worked before our eyes in the China of our day.

With this choice in mind, *China: The Hidden Miracle* could be seen as two books in one. It has two authors, who have written about different aspects of this great subject of China and her church, in different styles and with different but complementary purposes. One part of the book is the China story of a couple whom God took 'through fire and water', revealing His miraculous grace and power. The second part of the book gives historical perspective and spiritual understanding, relating these events to China's church in general and to the lives of Christians outside China.

As the two eyes in our head give us better vision by adding dimension and depth to our sight, so the two halves of this book offer two approaches to the same record. By doing so, they give us focus and depth into one of the most thrilling and challenging stories of our day – that of the Christian church in China.

In the first section of the book, you will rejoice at the evidence of God's love and power given to the ordinary people in China in our day. It is encouraging to know that the God who reached in amazing ways into the lives of these two ordinary people will also reach into our lives.

The second section of the book offers understanding and a perspective of those events, enabling you to see that this is not just a remote historical record, but a fact of life in China today. It will also help you to see how you can be involved in what today is still an ongoing narrative of the acts of God. You may prefer to understand the historical framework of such events before reading the events themselves. If so, first read chapter sixteen, which gives a brief historical understanding as to why the events that so influenced the lives of the Ye's came to pass.

'Who has believed our message and to whom has the arm of the Lord been revealed? He grew up before Him like a tender shoot, and like a root out of dry ground. He had no beauty or majesty to attract us to Him, nothing in His appearance that we should desire Him. He was despised and rejected by men, a man of sorrows, and familiar with suffering. Like one from whom men hide their faces He was despised, and we esteemed Him not. Surely He took up our infirmities and carried our sorrows, yet we considered Him stricken by God, smitten by Him, and afflicted.'

(Isaiah 53:1–4, NIV)

'Your beauty should not come from outward adornment, such as braided hair and the wearing of gold jewellery and fine clothes. Instead, it should be that of your inner self, the unfading beauty of a gentle and quiet spirit, which is of great worth in God's sight.' (1 Peter 3:3–4, NIV)

Chapter 1

Beginnings and Back Doors

With 1.15 billion people in China, selecting two of them to feature in a book could be a daunting task. What possible criteria could we use to narrow such an enormous number of potential candidates down to a mere few? Certainly the finalists would have to be unique. They would surely need to have distinguished themselves in some noteworthy field in order to rise above every other candidate. They could not be timid or self-effacing or their names would never become well-known. In short, they would have to be almost superhuman in every area of accomplishment.

The two people whose story is told here exhibit none of these qualities. From a human point of view, they are very ordinary people. They would not stand out in a crowded room, and no one would be attracted to them simply by their external appearance. Their 'extraordinariness' does not lie on the outside, but on the inside. And that is the story of the church in China – people who seem ordinary but who are full of extraordinary faith; a faith that allows them to grow and blossom in the midst of persecution, arrest, imprisonment, torture, and even death. The details of each believer's story may differ from village to village and from province to province, but suffering is invariably part of their testimony.

If that was all there was to their stories, however, no-one would want to read about them. But the couple whose story is told in these pages – as with so many believers in China –

have not only known suffering and persecution. They have known miraculous manifestations of the love of God leading to triumph and victory.

The experience of the couple whom we call the Ye's is just one of many that could be told. A real couple (although their names and certain details have been changed), they represent literally millions of Chinese Christians who have similarly served the Lord in ways that those of us outside China cannot imagine.

Ross Paterson first met the Ye's years ago when visiting a Christian friend in a town in southern China. The friend had spoken so highly of them that Ross planned an evening visit to meet them. A steep wooden staircase led the way to their second-floor apartment where amidst meagre surroundings the Ye's had prepared a magnificent meal for their western guest. Although the exact dishes they served are long forgotten, the warmth of their hospitality and the instand bond of Christian love remain vivid to this day.

The Ye's did not easily let their visitor go, and Ross too was reluctant to leave them. When he eventually did so, Mr Ye accompanied him to the place where he was staying. Both men knew it was dangerous for a Chinese Christian to be seen openly with a foreigner, yet neither wanted to part. The joy of that meeting has long lingered. The Ye's testimony was fragrant with the love and power of the Lord Jesus, rather than the sorrow or bitterness that we might expect from lives that had faced such crushing persecution. It was a rich blessing for Ross to be able to hear it.

There were many subjects discussed that night. One comment that remains very vivid is Mr Ye's explanation that he and his fellow believers in China never met in any building to worship Jesus unless the room had a back door. To those outside China, that seems an odd requirement. Yet for Christians inside China, who must constantly be on their guard against police entering the front door to break up a meeting, a back door escape route is a necessity.

Years later Elisabeth Farrell met the Ye's – this time under very different circumstances, as her part of the work on *China: The Hidden Miracle* began. As guests in her home, the Ye's brought countless hours of joy and laughter – in spite of the language barrier. Obviously uncomfortable with their roles as 'guests', they insisted on finding ways to serve – fixing a broken doorknob, walking the dog (they had been forced to leave theirs behind in China), and making dozens of 'jiao zi' dumplings.

One afternoon while Elisabeth was working on the book, illustrator Gloria Kohlmann and her husband Jim, joined her and the Ye's for a meal. Sitting in a neighbourhood Chinese restaurant, the table laden with dishes, it was almost impossible to imagine that this joyful laughing couple had been through so much. Finally, the conversation took a sobering turn. Jim asked Mr Ye how he endured the trials that he had faced. There was barely a pause, because this man who had suffered so much for his faith already knew the answer. 'God did not give me faith to believe or even hope I'd be free by a certain date,' Mr Ye said. 'He simply gave me faith to hold on day by day.'

This is the 'ordinary' couple with such an 'extraordinary' faith that we invite you to meet.

Chapter 2

Two Miraculous Healings

'For this child I prayed, and the Lord has granted me my petition which I asked of Him. Therefore I also have lent him to the Lord; as long as he lives he shall be lent to the Lord.'
(1 Samuel 1:27–28)

Exhausted and hungry, Chen Guihua shifted her tired body on the hard wooden hospital bench. She told herself that she had to stay awake, because if she didn't pray for her son, who would? She looked down at the still figure on the cot next to her. It was the third time in her son's six years on earth that he had faced tuberculosis, and this time it seemed he no longer had the strength to fight it. Ye Enshi was deep in a coma and slipping away before his mother's very eyes.

For days, Chen Guihua had kept a constant vigil by her son's bed, not stopping to eat or return home to care for her other children. Around the clock she stayed at his side, praying that God would heal him and spare his young life. Across the crowded ward, she could see the doctors conferring among themselves. Surely there was something else they could try, she thought. Surely they hadn't given up hope that her precious son would jump and laugh again.

Had Chen Guihua been able to hear what the doctors were saying, she would have realised they had indeed given up hope. In fact, they were convinced that it was only a matter of hours before Enshi died, and they were already making plans to call the morgue. Chen Guihua watched them intently, then turned her attention back to her son. 'Lord,' she prayed with desperation, 'don't let him die.' Warm tears slipped from her eyes and dropped onto her son's limp body. 'If You give me back his life,' she added softly, 'I'll dedicate him to You. Just don't let him die.'

When Chen Guihua opened her eyes, she was surprised to see a nurse standing over her – not with medication, but with a bowl of steaming chicken soup. 'It's for you,' the nurse told her, 'because if you don't eat, you're going to die also.'

Even the nurse had given up hope, Chen Guihua thought, but she refused to. She stirred the rich broth, fragrant with the scent of ginger, green onions and sesame, and blew softly to cool it. But instead of drinking it herself, she carefully spooned the liquid into Enshi's parched mouth. What happened next completely shocked both Chen Guihua and the watching nurse. First there was slight movement from Enshi's eyelids, then they popped open and Enshi clearly cried out, 'Mama! Mama!'

They were the words Chen Guihua had begged God to hear again. 'He's alive!' she yelled to anyone who would listen. 'My child has come back to life!' Across the room, one of the doctors heard the commotion and ran to Enshi's cot. The astonished expression on his face said that he was as shocked as anyone to find the boy awake and talking. Within a few days, the doctor signed the papers for Enshi's release and sent him home completely healed.

Only then did his mother tell him how she had prayed for his healing, and how she had told God that if he lived she would dedicate his life to the Lord. His grandfather added that he, too, had prayed the very same prayers on the day Enshi was healed. Even at such a young age, Enshi knew God had touched him, and he agreed with his mother and grandfather that he would spend his life serving God.

But it wasn't long before Enshi understood the reality of that vow, and he quickly decided to revise his plans. After some thought, he came up with a new goal: to be an athlete

– the best there ever was. But which sport should he concentrate on, he wondered? As he watched his friends swimming in the ponds and rivers near his home, he thought perhaps that was the sport he should pursue, but there was only one problem. He had no idea how to swim, and there was no one to teach him. A minor problem, Enshi thought, because he could easily teach himself – and he chose a Sunday morning to learn. Of course it meant skipping church, but what was more important? So while his parents headed for church, Enshi headed for the river.

It didn't matter that there was no one else around. Enshi plunged right in. It wasn't long, however, before he realised he was not only in deep water but also in deep trouble. The more he thrashed about trying to stay afloat, the quicker he sank to the bottom. The frigid darkness of the river surrounded him and he couldn't even tell which direction was up and which was down. Fighting fear and panic, Enshi suddenly remembered where his parents were at the moment – and where he was supposed to be had he listened to them. If God was really God, Enshi thought, He could be in two places at once, so he cried out to Him for help.

All of a sudden in the midst of the dark murky water surrounding him, a bright light appeared. Enshi somehow knew that he was to stand on it – and as he did so, he instantly found himself in shallow water. Without wasting a moment trying to figure out what had happened, Enshi pulled himself out of the river and ran straight for the church where his parents were attending the service. Although the meeting was half over, he heard enough to convince himself that God was real. The God who saved him from drowning earlier that morning was the same God who was in this church, and Enshi made up his mind to serve Him no matter what.

And he did – for a while. But once again the vow he spoke in a moment of desperation was somehow forgotten. One afternoon while sitting in the branches of his favourite willow tree, he told himself that this business of dedicating his life to the Lord was his parents' idea, not his own. Enshi had other plans for his young life. He stared at the upper branches of the tree and decided this was the day to explore the ones that seemed to brush the clouds. Higher and higher he climbed until he found himself inching along fragile limbs that could no longer support the weight of his body.

Suddenly a loud *crack!* broke his reverie as the branch gave way and sent Enshi tumbling to the hard ground far below him. The excruciating pain in his arm jarred him back to his senses and he knew he had dislocated a bone. Enshi didn't dare tell his parents, so he hobbled home and turned to the only person he could tell: Jesus. Instead of turning His back on the boy who had turned his back on Him, the Lord touched Enshi's arm and instantly healed it. His parents never knew, and Enshi made up his mind that this time his days of running from God were really over.

His commitment to the Lord became even stronger when his mother developed a lung disease that had already killed many people in their county. Enshi overheard people in the village saying that nobody knew how to cure the disease – not with medication or herbs. There was nothing to do, it seemed, but to wait for death to claim yet another victim. Yet his mother refused to concede defeat, and whenever Enshi visited her in the hospital, he was the one who went away encouraged.

'Keep on praying and go to church,' she would tell him. 'And remember, I've dedicated you to the Lord, so obey His commands and be a good servant to Him.' Enshi prayed as hard as he knew how to pray – and one day his father told him a miracle had happened. His mother was coming home completely healed. Needless to say, there was a celebration among the believers in the village who knew that God had spared Chen Guihua's life. Joyfully, she explained what had happened.

'I simply told the Lord that there was too much I wanted to do for Him on earth and I couldn't die yet,' she said. 'I told Him I needed ten more years of life.'

One night while she was in the hospital, she went on to

explain, she became so delirious that she could feel herself going in and out of consciousness. Suddenly, right there in her hospital room, an angel appeared to her. He didn't say a word, but simply held up both hands with all ten fingers extended.

'I knew God was saying He was granting my request for another ten years of life!' laughed Chen Guihua. And as she had promised the Lord, she worked even harder than she had before.

Enshi was so impressed by his mother's healing and renewed commitment to serve God that he, too, resolved to devote himself to the Lord's service even more than he had before. The best way to do that, he decided, would be to help his father in his ministerial duties beginning with cleaning the church building every week. At first, Enshi's enthusiasm for his new calling carried him through, and he faithfully showed up at church week by week, sweeping and dusting and cleaning until every bench shimmered with polish and every window sparkled in the glistening China sun.

But in spite of his earnest determination, it wasn't long before Enshi's heartfelt dedication to the Lord once again wavered. Oh, he still wanted to serve God, he told himself, but maybe there was another way to do it. One day while watching his friends play the violin, piano and other instruments, he came up with a plan. The best way to serve the Lord, he decided, would be to become a musician. And to really serve God well, he wouldn't be just any musician, but the most famous musician in the entire world. Enshi decided the violin offered him the best opportunity to serve God in an appropriate manner, and so he began lessons. His teachers encouraged him and actually said he was quite a gifted student.

But God had other plans for Enshi, in spite of the talent he exhibited in the school orchestra. At first Enshi thought the breathing problems he experienced whenever he put the violin to his chin were just a passing coincidence. But soon the pain grew so intense that he had to reluctantly accept defeat and make the difficult decision to give up the violin – and with it his plans of becoming the world's greatest violinist.

Enshi realised he had been outmanoeuvred and out-smarted by Someone a lot bigger than himself. No matter what he did, it seemed that God had other plans for his life and there wasn't a thing he could do about it. Enshi was beginning to taste for himself how strong God's love was for him, even when he gave in to sin and temptation. The words of his favourite psalm, Psalm 23, became more and more real to him in these days as he saw for himself that the Lord was indeed his Shepherd, faithfully leading him.

Chapter 3

Three Conditions

'To everything there is a season, a time for every purpose under heaven ... a time to plant, and a time to pluck what is planted.' (Ecclesiastes 3:1–2)

'All right, Lord,' Enshi said reluctantly. 'I'll go to a seminary if You really want me to ... but You've got to meet three conditions first.'

When Enshi graduated from high school, seminary was about the furthest thing from his mind. A bright gregarious 17 year old, he was active in a host of school activities and had dozens of friends. Like them, Enshi knew what he wanted to do with his life – or thought he did – and had his mind set on being an engineer. University entrance exams were right around the corner, and every spare moment of Enshi's free time was devoted to preparing for them.

But Enshi's father, it seemed, had different plans for his son. He wanted him to go to a seminary, become a minister like he was, and spend his life serving God. The idea didn't seem nearly as appealing to Enshi as it did to his father. They'd had the same discussion countless times in the past few months, and it always ended with Enshi declaring emphatically that there were many ways to serve God, and he could do it best by becoming an engineer.

His father wouldn't let the subject drop, but Enshi had no intention of listening to his voice or the other persistent one that he often heard when he sat quietly in his father's church. It wasn't until the morning he filled out the application forms for the university entrance exams that he realised that he might indeed have to change his plans.

In the days just before the Cultural Revolution ripped China to shreds, Christians were not allowed to attend university, putting Enshi in a quandary. Increasingly the government was adopting policies hostile to Christians, and young students like Enshi faced the brunt of their hatred. Enshi knew that if he lied on the application form and said he wasn't a Christian, he couldn't live with himself. Yet if he admitted he was a Christian, all hopes of his future as an engineer would end on the spot. There was only one way he could respond, so he never finished filling out the forms. Instead he tried to figure out what he was going to do with the rest of his life.

Finally, when all other doors seemed tightly shut, Enshi faced the fact that maybe God did want him to go to a seminary. At least they wouldn't throw him out for being a Christian. Enshi examined his options and decided seminary wasn't the worst thing he could do. When he looked at available seminaries, however, he discovered that his choices were considerably limited. In the mid 1950's, as today, seminaries in China were all regulated by the Three Self Patriotic Movement (TSPM), a government religious organisation that controls virtually every aspect of church life.

Although technically a spiritual organisation, the TSPM was in fact highly political in its top leadership. These men and women were often more committed to pleasing their Marxist masters than to obedience to the Bible. Their position is perhaps most easily summed up in their self-confessed credo, 'Love your country, love your religion' – in that order. For those who sought to put Christ before Caesar, there were harsh penalities, sometimes even directly from the church leaders.*

Enshi knew that the seminaries were a major target for

---

* For a more complete explanation of the TSPM, please refer to Chapter 16.

this political activity. Yet he realised he had no choice. There were no other schools anywhere in China where one could receive theological training, so he continued the application process. At the same time, however, he gave God one last chance to change His mind. Enshi told Him that he would go to seminary if He met three conditions first. One, he needed permission from the seminary. Two, he needed money to attend. And three, he needed someone to meet him in the city where the seminary was located because he didn't know a single person there. Enshi smiled to himself as he realised that the conditions were impossible even for God to meet. Once and for all, he would prove to himself – and to his father – that there had to be another way.

In a matter of days Enshi had an admission form in his hand – the 'gift' of a friend who didn't tell Enshi he was obtaining it for him. Enshi reluctantly filled out the form, mailed it to the school, and to his amazement received a response that he was accepted. The first condition was met ... but there was still the problem of finances.

Suddenly it seemed like everyone Enshi knew started handing him money – a little here from someone in his church, a little there from someone in his town, even people who didn't know of his plans would come up to him in the crowded market–place and give him a few coins. Slowly the donations added up, and to Enshi's astonishment, the day he was to leave for seminary he had exactly the amount he needed – not any more, not any less.

Even Enshi – a sceptic from the beginning – had to admit that God was saying seminary was what He had in mind all the time. Enshi packed his belongings, said goodbye to his family and friends, and waited for the final condition to be met. A few days later he stood on the deck of a ship that slowly steamed its way upriver to the city where the seminary was located. Below him in tiny boats bobbing on the water, a fisherman was pulling his cormorant bird in and out of the river. The bird would dive into the water for fish, but just as he tried to fly away with his catch, his owner would tug on the rope around his neck and pull him back into the boat. Enshi had to laugh as he watched the comical bird, because he knew that he too was trying to fly away, but God invariably pulled him back in.

Finally the ship arrived at its destination and Enshi once again laughed as he heard a voice on the loudspeaker announce the name of the docking place: 'Toward the Gate of Heaven'. It was obvious that God had organised this entire trip and was pointing him 'toward Heaven'.

The captain deftly manoeuvred the ship to its docking place, and Enshi wondered how God was going to meet the third condition. He scanned the dock for a friendly face, but saw no one he knew – and no one who seemed to know him. Yet he remembered how God had met his first two conditions in ways he never could have imagined in his craziest dreams, and he just accepted the fact that something miraculous was about to happen. Enshi had barely taken his first step off the ship and on to the swaying wooden dock when he heard a young woman's voice that seemed to rise above all the others in the crowd.

'You! You there!' she called.

Enshi looked around to see whom she was talking to, but no one seemed to be paying attention to her.

'You!' the woman called again, this time looking directly at him. 'Are you Ye Enshi? I've come to take you to the seminary.'

From that moment on, seminary became an adventure for Enshi.

On the walk to the seminary, the young woman cheerfully told him all about his new school – what he would be studying, who would be teaching him, and how he would be joining students from all over China who had dedicated their lives to serving the Lord in the midst of the tumultuous times their country was facing. With each step, Enshi grew more and more excited about what was in store for him in the coming weeks, but the fire of his enthusiasm was quickly snuffed out when he got his first glimpse of the seminary buildings. The place was in complete shambles. Everywhere Enshi looked, he saw doors falling off their hinges, classrooms in disrepair, and walls covered with peeling paint.

Enshi knew he was required to raise his own tuition and support, but he was appalled to learn the seminary was virtually without any funds at all. Each day was a test of faith for students and staff, who told Enshi that they chose to look at the difficult times as an opportunity to put into practice what they were learning in class.

'Our school is administered by the Lord,' the president told them over and over again.

Students and staff alike shared whatever meagre funds and food they had. Whenever Enshi's family sent him some money from their own limited supply, he would quickly share it with the others. The school owned a cow that gave enough milk each day to enable students to give some to anyone who was sick in town, keep some for themselves, and sell the rest to support the school. But there were times when no food or drink was to be found anywhere on any shelf in the seminary. Once when there was not even a spoonful of salt or a single grain of rice – and no money to buy any – the president told the students to kneel together and petition the 'Administrator of the school'.

Enshi joined the others in fervent prayer that was often echoed by the sounds of stomachs gurgling with hunger. Just as one student was making a particularly eloquent plea, the door to the room popped open and in ran the cook.

'Hallelujah!' he shouted, triumphantly holding a basket filled with food. 'Someone has brought us vegetables and rice!'

Another meal was put on the table through faith.

And so Enshi learned about trusting God for every meal. He also learned to trust Him to meet every other need too. One overcast morning, for example, he had to go to a meeting in a nearby town. The boat ticket he would need for the trip was five cents – exactly five cents more than he had in his pocket. Alone in his room as the grey clouds prepared to unleash a torrent of rain on him the moment he set foot outside the door, Enshi prayed and asked God for five cents. From deep within, he heard a voice whisper, 'Don't be afraid. Just show up at the dock.'

With surprising boldness for someone whose pockets were completely empty, Enshi sang the entire way to the dock in anticipation of the miracle God would have waiting there for him. Just as he rounded the bend toward the dock, he saw a friend furiously waving and shouting at him. As Enshi got closer he realised that in his friend's hand were two small pieces of paper – a boat ticket for himself and another for Enshi. The friend, it seemed, just happened to have an extra five cents that day, which the Lord told him to use for a boat ticket for Enshi.

As difficult times spread throughout China, life at the seminary became more and more difficult for staff and students alike. Because the seminary was controlled by the TSPM, the students were required to attend indoctrination meetings filled with Marxist-Leninist thought. The classes droned on interminably, and each month it seemed a new one was added to an already crowded schedule. Soon Enshi couldn't keep up with his regular class work because most of his time was occupied with political courses.

The financial situation at school also seemed to go from bad to worse. One by one, the students lost what little support they had. Then their president died. One day even the cow died. Finally the government decided to close the school entirely and send all the students to another seminary also controlled by the TSPM. It was obvious to Enshi and the other students that it was the Lord, not the government, who was really closing the door and cutting off their support because He didn't want them to be involved with a compromise anymore. Why should they be enrolled in a seminary to learn the ways of the Kingdom when much of what they were learning were the ways of a communist and atheistic government?

God had built the seminary. He had caused it to grow. And now He was shutting it down. One by one the students left. Enshi was the very last one to go.

Chapter 4

A Fearless Decision

'Behold! My Servant whom I uphold, My Elect One in whom My soul delights! I have put My Spirit upon Him ... to open blind eyes, to bring out prisoners from the prison, those who sit in darkness from the prison house.'   (Isaiah 42:1, 7)

Enshi studied the faces of the dozens of people around the crowded room who were packed like geese in a bamboo basket on market day. There wasn't a square inch of space not used to its fullest. Men and women were shoulder to shoulder on straw mats on the floor, lined up on wooden benches, balanced on top of desks, under tables, even crowded around the feet of the minister, whose words they took in like those who had not had a glass of cool water in weeks.

As Enshi watched their faces, he grew more and more angry. Why wasn't everyone allowed to be here, he wanted to know. Why did the government say young people could not attend church?

The injustice of the new law made Enshi seethe with anger, and rather than concentrating on the words of the minister, he worked on a plan to defy the new law. Yes, it was illegal, and yes, he could be in deep trouble with the government, but at this point he didn't care. He was tired of the officials telling Christians what they could and couldn't study, when they could and couldn't meet, and where they could and couldn't congregate.

At the end of the meeting, he pulled the minister aside and told him he was volunteering to lead a Bible study in his home for high school and university students. The minister's first reaction was shock as he realised the implication of the move – not only for the young people and Enshi, but for the entire church. But he also admired the fearlessness of the man standing before him.

The minister started to warn Enshi to be careful, but it was obvious Enshi had already made up his mind. When it came down to a choice between following God or the government, there was no question in Enshi's mind whom he would choose. Long ago he had settled the issue of Whom he was serving with his life. He had given up dreams of becoming a musician and an engineer in order to follow God. He had even passed up marrying any of the dozens of eligible young women in his village in order to be able to marry the woman he felt God telling him was to be his chosen wife, a laughing joy-filled beauty named Huiliang. He saw in her a quality that he didn't see in the other young women he had met – a love of the Lord that seemed to defy circumstances. When he confided in her about his plans to lead a home Bible Study, she had enthusiastically backed his decision – knowing full well the danger that such a move could bring. Yes, Enshi thought, it was only a matter of time before he asked Huiliang to be his wife.

And so Enshi began his Bible study for any young person who wanted to come. As a further sign of his resolve not to bow to government pressure, Enshi launched his study with Revelation, one of the books of the Bible that the government had declared was illegal for Christians to study – even those belonging to the official TSPM churches. Enshi knew that Bible books such as Revelation and Daniel contained vivid descriptions of the End Times, which no doubt made communists and atheists nervous.

Week after week, young people crowded into Enshi's family home. Because they came from all over the city,

Enshi didn't know each of them personally, and with so many guests each week he never knew if someone was there with the sole purpose of turning him in to the government for illegal activities. The young people, too, were in danger, and were constantly on guard, praying that God would protect them not only during the meetings, but also when they were at school, at work, and even in their homes. Many had parents who were not Christians, and it would be all too easy to leave a book or paper lying around the house that would result in a stern lecture about the glories of communism and the foolishness of Christianity.

In spite of their caution. Enshi and Huiliang knew it was only a matter of time before someone was caught. That 'someone', it turned out, was Chen Haoming, a young man who worked in a nearby factory. Six months after the Bible study began, Chen Haoming received a message from his work committee. His presence was required at a meeting in Shanghai, he was told, and his superior handed him a train ticket and told him to go to the railway station immediately. Although the circumstances surrounding the sudden meeting seemed suspicious, there was nothing Chen Haoming could do about it. He wouldn't dare disobey the work committee or his superiors, so he reluctantly followed their instructions.

Before the train even arrived in Shanghai, Chen Haoming realised his caution was well founded. While the train was rattling its way through emerald green rice fields and silvery watering holes, a group of men burst into the car where Chen Haoming sat silently praying and arrested him for participating in an illegal Bible study. Without a hearing or a trial, he was forcibly taken back to his hometown and immediately thrown into a prison directly across the street from Enshi's house.

With such a vantage point, it wasn't long before government officials began to investigate others attending the Bible study meetings. More and more young people were arrested – all on the grounds that they were involved in illegal religious activities. Officials angrily accused them of having their own doctrine that was against that of the communist party.

To the surprise of the officials, however, the continual persecution and arrests did nothing to stop the meetings, so the government turned to other means. High school students who attended the Bible study found they were denied entrance to universities. University students were assigned the worst jobs upon graduation. Many other Christians simply disappeared. Enshi knew it was only a matter of time before he too, would face arrest.

One evening as he returned from an out-of-town trip, a government official ordered him to attend an indoctrination meeting, one of the many held week in and week out to try to instil Marxist–Leninist teaching in the minds of China's people. Something told Enshi he shouldn't go to the meeting, but he knew he didn't really have a choice. He told his fiancée, Huiliang, that he wouldn't be more than a few hours, but in his heart he suspected that he, too, might be thrown into prison on trumped up charges.

And sure enough, as soon as he arrived at the meeting, he was surrounded by police, arrested, and informed he was being sent to prison – the same one where his friend, Chen Haoming, was being held. After a stay of indeterminate length, he would be moved to a rural area in the mountains where he would be forced to do hard labour designed to 're-educate and rebuild' him, and rid him once and for all of his 'counter-revolutionary' religious beliefs.

The worst part of the ordeal was that his captors forbade him to contact Huiliang and tell her what was happening. He could only pray that one of the other people in the room at the time of his arrest would tell her what had happened.

In spite of being locked in a crowded prison cell and facing an uncertain future, Enshi actually began to get excited by the prospect of what God might have in store for him. Behind these very same walls, he knew, were Chen Haoming and many other young men from his Bible study. Enshi would somehow try to find them and encourage them to remain strong in their faith. Although he was not allowed to talk to other prisoners, no one said anything about singing. So one morning not long after his arrest, he took a deep breath, opened his mouth, and started to sing every hymn he could think of at the top of his voice in order to attract the attention of other Christians. But it was a guard whose attention was attracted, and he told Enshi to be quiet or he would have to restrain him with ropes to ensure his silence.

Enshi decided to try another approach. He stood quietly by the tiny window in his cell and sang softly. Over and over again he barely whispered the notes to first one song, then another. Finally he heard it – someone was singing with him! Only a fellow believer would know the songs he was singing and Enshi was overjoyed to realise there was another believer nearby whom he could encourage by singing. It was none other than Chen Haoming, the first young person to be arrested from the Bible study.

As more and more people were arrested – many for 'crimes' as nebulous as Enshi's – the already overcrowded prison became almost unbearable. Finally Enshi and dozens of other prisoners were transferred to a labour camp in a rural, mountainous area of the country. The conditions there were even more horrendous than they had been in the city prison. The cells were filthy, prisoners suffered from diseases of the most abhorrent nature, their mail was read, their belongings searched, and day in and day out they were required to perform hard labour while heavily armed soldiers kept a careful watch.

In 1960, famine spread through the entire province, and conditions in the camp deteriorated even further. Prisoners ate anything they could find – roots, ferns, even frogs – but the lack of nutritious food coupled with back-breaking work meant their health quickly degenerated. Many times, in fact, Enshi awoke in the morning to find that the man next to him had died during the night.

While many prisoners tried to escape these appalling conditions, Enshi and the other Christians accepted where God had placed them, knowing they could use the opportunity to spread the Gospel behind bars. The guards knew they were Christians and consequently knew they would not escape, so when they chose prisoners for work assignments in the deserted mountainous regions, it was Enshi and the other Christians who were always at the top of the list.

Although it was a luxury to be free from watchful eyes even for a few hours, it was far from a vacation in the sun. Deep in the woods of the mountains, they had to scour the cold, lifeless ground searching for roots to bring back to the camp for the other prisoners to eat. Normally roots would be soaked in water for a week to make them edible, but because of the extent of the famine and the extreme hunger of prisoners, no one wanted to wait seven days for a meal. They might be dead by then. And so the roots were consumed virtually raw. They were bitter and almost impossible to digest, but at least they filled their empty stomachs, however temporarily.

In spite of the demanding nature of the mountain work, the guards recognised that it was nonetheless a choice assignment, so they made it as difficult as possible to qualify for it. Each prisoner had to collect 100 pounds of roots everyday, or they couldn't go out the next day. Enshi and another Christian, Lin Luoying, a medical doctor, knew the requirement was almost impossible to meet. There was no way humanly possible that a healthy man could collect 100 pounds of roots a day, much less a man on the verge of death. In addition, Enshi and Lin Luoying were both born and bred in cities, and they didn't have the vaguest idea how to locate roots, dig them, or cut them – or how to do it as fast as possible.

But they did know how to pray, so they began each day asking the Lord to give them 'wisdom for finding roots' and to help them fulfil the 100-pound requirement so that they could spend time in the relative freedom of the mountains. There they could talk, sing, pray, share Scriptures, and encourage each other to continue in spite of their overwhelming circumstances. The mountain furloughs also enabled them to buy beef from local peasants, cook it in the mountains, and take it back to prison for the other Christians. Because they knew they would be searched upon their return, they hid the meat in bottles, praying it would not be found.

But in spite of the contraband meat, Lin Luoying's health continued to wane and he was no longer able to collect 100 pounds of roots a day. So Enshi made a decision. In order for Lin Luoying to continue joining him on the work assignments in the mountains, Enshi would have to collect enough roots for the two of them. While Lin Luoying stayed by the river washing clothes and praying, Enshi worked at a frantic pace and somehow managed to collect enough tree roots for a double load – 200 pounds in all. Day after day the miracle was repeated: Enshi not only had enough roots by the end of the day to share with Lin Luoying, but he also collected them quickly enough so that he and his friend had time to pray before they were due back in camp.

No matter what unreasonable demands the guards put on them, God, it seemed, helped them in ways that defied rational explanation.

Chapter 5

What the Enemy Meant for Evil

'Joseph said to them..., "You meant evil against me; but God meant it for good, in order to bring it about as it is this day, to save many people alive."'
(Genesis 50:19–20)

Enshi carefully manoeuvred his way along the narrow path, knowing that one wrong move could endanger not only his own life but the lives of the men behind him who were watching his every step. To their right stretched swells of tall parched grass as far as the eye could see – dry, crisp, and rippling in the wind. To their left roared a brush fire, invigorated by the wind and searing everything in its path. For Enshi and the men behind him, the hazards were all part of a day's work in the labour camp.

'Be careful Enshi,' warned the man directly behind him. 'The wind is changing and it might blow the flames across the path.'

If it did, they knew that in a matter of seconds they could all be engulfed by flames, and the prison guards watching them from a safe distance would do nothing to rescue them. With deliberate and measured care, Enshi chose his steps through the obstacle course, taking a moment to glance to his left and shudder at the closeness of the blaze.

'Watch out!' cried the man behind him. In the split second Enshi used to look at the flames, he failed to see a rock partially hidden in the dusty path in front of him.

Before he knew what happened, he tripped, lost his balance, and fell – tumbling directly into the flames.

The screams of those behind him echoed above the sound of the raging fire – not so much because of what had happened to Enshi, but because the other men saw what he didn't. Just as he fell, the flames on the left side of the path leapt in front of him and ignited the grass to his right, creating a burning bridge that was not more than a few feet from where he lay.

'If that fall had not stopped you,' the man behind him said, 'we'd all be in those flames.'

As Enshi quickly scrambled to his feet, he realised that God had not only miraculously intervened to spare their lives, but that he had not been burned – in spite of rolling through the burning grass. Like the three young Hebrew men in the furnace, he did not even have the smell of fire upon him.

For those in prison, life was a constant hazard, never knowing when death might come. Yet believers had the assurance of Psalm 23:4,

> *'Though I walk through the valley of the shadow of death, I will fear no evil; for You are with me; Your rod and Your staff they comfort me.'*

Enshi saw God's miraculous protection from death again and again. One of his assignments in prison, for example, was digging coal and carrying it back to camp. Each prisoner was required to carry 100-pound loads at a time. The weight made the job difficult enough, but the path back to camp required the prisoners to cross a river by walking across a narrow log. One slip of the foot or a shift in weight of the coal and they would be in the river and far downstream before anyone could do anything about it.

Enshi had had a lot of experiences in life, but nothing he could think of had prepared him for this. While he waited for other prisoners to cross the rickety bridge, he prayed and asked the Lord to give him wisdom about how to make the trip. As he finished praying, he noticed that the other men had a certain way of carrying their loads that enabled them to use the weight to balance themselves on the log. When his turn came around, he took a deep breath, stepped out onto the log, and tried to imitate the way the others had crossed. Sure enough, he found it was actually easier to walk with the load than without it because the weight helped him maintain his balance. It was as if once again God had saved him from death – this time by sending His 'rod and staff' to help him cross the river.

Another time while Enshi was on a work assignment collecting bamboo in the mountains, he accidentally grabbed a stalk that just happened to have a poisonous snake curled around it. As soon as Enshi touched the cold, clammy skin, he knew it was too late to pull back. His hand was close enough to the snake's protruding fangs for him to be bitten in a split second – and die before anyone ever found him. But instead of biting him, the snake inexplicably slunk off in the opposite direction.

Yet another time he was assigned to a prison crew carving a road through a mountainous region. One day the Lord gave him a clear vision of men digging into the side of a cliff that was about to fall. The vision was so vivid that Enshi let out an ear-piercing scream. Fifteen men ran to his side to see what had happened – and as they did, more than 5,000 pounds of dirt and rock fell exactly where they had been standing. Everyone escaped except for one man. The others furiously began to dig him out from the enormous pile, knowing it was impossible for a man to survive such a burial. Yet when they finally located him, he was still breathing and suffered only minor injuries. Among the men who were saved that day were non-believers – who had to admit that the God whom Enshi prayed to all the time had indeed saved their lives.

No matter what the enemy sent their way for evil, God invariably turned it for good.

Chapter 6

Sugarcane, Bamboo, and Real Gold

'The wicked covet the catch of evil men, but the root of the righteous yields fruit.'　　　　(Proverbs 12:12)

Enshi waited silently behind the pile of rotting fabric. The dampness of the prison storeroom aggravated his weakened condition, and he steadied himself with one hand while gripping a long stick with the other.

A year of prison life and a diet of bitter roots that even pigs and dogs refused to eat had left the young and once energetic man close to death. In fact, only a few weeks earlier Enshi had become so weak from the heavy labour and lack of decent food that he ended up in the prison hospital. Although there was no medicine to treat him, there was a little extra food in the hospital – particularly vegetables – set aside for sick prisoners. Meal after meal, Enshi ate anything that was put in front of him. The food was a far cry from the fragrant dishes that his precious Huiliang used to prepare for him whenever he would visit her at her parents' home, but he was grateful to the Lord for the unexpected bounty.

Finally the prison doctors decided that Enshi was well enough to be released from the hospital, in spite of the fact that he still felt as if he was sitting on death's doorstep. At twenty-seven years old, he knew that unless something changed, he would wind up in the same condition as the men whose bodies were carried out of the bunks in the morning – dead from malnutrition, exhaustion, and exposure to the bitter cold weather.

Now, waiting quietly in the dank storeroom, Enshi knew God was once again providing for him. It wasn't exactly a gourmet meal that might be served in the finest restaurants in Peking, but at this point Enshi's growling stomach was far from particular.

With what little strength he could muster, Enshi gripped the stick and silently watched as his next meal crept in and out of the heaps of fabric. When the moment was right, with one swift move, he lashed the stick through the air and across the neck of a large black rat.

Elsewhere in the storeroom, a small group of fellow prisoners cheered Enshi's success as they too, thrashed at the hundreds of rats scurrying in the room's dark corners.

Normally, prisoners were forbidden to eat the rats, in spite of the fact that the dark furry creatures darting everywhere were the only meat that most prisoners had seen in months. But in a surprising token of generosity, the prison leader had not only given Enshi and the other Christians permission to eat any rats they caught, but had also told them they were allowed to use the prison's kitchen facilities to cook them.

As grateful as the prisoners were for this unexpected luxury, they knew that the filthy rats could very well carry diseases. Yet they knew that the rats were also God's miraculous provision for them when other prisoners were subsisting on watered-down broth.

And so before they had a chance to change their minds, they quickly skinned the thirty animals they caught and cut off their heads, tails, and feet. Fighting back nausea, they cleaned out the organs and threw what was left into a pot of boiling water. As they stirred the soup, they prayed that God would remove any disease that the rats carried, remembering how He told Peter that it was alright to eat food that he considered unholy and unclean,

> *'Rise, Peter, kill and eat ... What God has cleansed you must not call common.'*   (Acts 10:13, 15)

Finally the moment came when someone had to taste the meaty stew to make sure it was edible. Zhang Pingshan volunteered for the assignment. The others knew that if he spat it out – or perhaps even fell over dead – their gourmet dinner would have to be thrown away, no matter how hungry they were. Zhang Pingshan found a spoon in the dirty cabinets, wiped it on his shirt, and gingerly scooped up a bit of the liquid. The others watched as he hesitantly tasted it – a sip at a time.

Finally he made his pronouncement, 'It's delicious! Even better than chicken soup!'

The words were no sooner out of his mouth than the other men began to fill their own enamel bowls and hungrily gulp down the unusual feast. Many of them were from the city and some had never even seen a rat before, much less eaten one. Yet they knew that God had provided this unexpected meal for them – the most nutritious they had eaten in months. Three more times they caught rats in the prison storeroom, boiled them, and gratefully devoured them. And very quickly, Enshi, like the others, began to regain his strength.

Once again, the Lord had met all their needs, in ways that did not require them to disobey the rules. In prison, there were plenty of opportunities to get what one needed if one was willing to resort to devious means to do it. But as Christians, Enshi and the others knew they couldn't compromise their Christian beliefs, no matter how famished they were. If they waited for God to move instead of trusting in their own devices, He would invariably show them what they could eat and exactly where to find it.

Once, for example, Enshi was told he was being assigned to hard labour in the nearby sugarcane fields. There, hundreds of prisoners worked from early in the morning until late in the evening carrying heavy stalks of cane. As weak as Enshi was, he knew God had a plan when He assigned him to the new task, and he patiently waited to find out what it was. When he arrived at the work site, the prison guard told him that, like the other prisoners, he was not allowed to take any sugar back to the camp. The penalty for stealing even a small amount of sugar was a severe beating. But, the guard told him he was allowed to eat anything he wanted while he was in the fields.

Enshi guessed that the guard figured one prisoner couldn't eat very much sugar, but Enshi knew better. Refined sugar, such as the kind found in most kitchens, would not necessarily have been a help to Enshi's failing health, but unrefined sugar found in the freshly cut sugarcane stalks was just what Enshi's weakened body needed. Day after day, he chewed on the sweet stalks whenever he could and the energy he received helped him regain even more of his lost strength.

But the sugarcane assignment was not to last forever. Once he was stronger, he was reassigned to a new and much more demanding task: cutting bamboo in the mountains. Here God provided for him once again. As soon as Enshi and the other prisoners arrived at the mountain site early each morning, they waited for the guards to be out of sight and then quickly went into action. While one person searched the trees and bushes for wild nuts, another dug a hole and built a fire inside it. As soon as the ground was hot, they filled the hole with nuts, covered them with dirt, and went about the difficult task of gathering bamboo. Late in the day they would return to find the nuts warm and toasted – the perfect protein-packed meal for them to eat as they carried their heavy loads back to camp.

Each time Enshi was reassigned to a new task, he waited to see God's plan – and how the Lord would allow him to do something legally that normally the guards would not permit. His next assignment was at a large factory where he was told his 're-education' would continue. Occasionally he was allowed to leave the factory after work, but always, he knew, another prisoner would be ordered to follow him. Not all the men in prison were there for political reasons.

Many were common criminals – thieves, murderers and other violent men. But to the prison officials, Christians were criminals also, and the men were all thrown together in the same cells. More often than not, these common criminals were the men chosen to follow Enshi whenever he left the factory.

On one such excursion, Enshi was astounded to learn that the guards were actually giving him some free time. He decided the best way to enjoy this unexpected luxury was to visit a believer who lived in the same village. The fellowship that the two men enjoyed that afternoon was an encouragement to them both, and Enshi returned to the prison factory with his faith renewed and his spirits soaring. As soon as he walked through the factory gates, however, he was immediately taken to a special room for questioning. The prison officials, he quickly learned, knew exactly how he had spent his afternoon.

'Are you *still* a believer in Jesus?' the head official demanded, furious that his attempts to re-educate Enshi were getting nowhere.

Enshi did not have to think twice before he answered. 'Yes,' he replied 'I'm still a believer!'

Another official shook his head with pity at the sight of this young man who refused to back down from his fanciful beliefs. 'How stubborn you are!' he said, pounding the table in frustration.

Enshi knew what his 'stubbornness' would cost him, but he also knew that in a way he was the free man while they were the prisoners. They were being held captive by the bonds of atheism and sin, and he held the keys to release them into the same salvation – the same freedom – that he had experienced. He took a deep breath and began to tell them exactly why he was 'still a believer in Jesus'. He told them how his Father in heaven loved him so much that He sent His only son to die for him. Because Jesus took his place on the cross – a place that was rightfully and legally Enshi's – Enshi would not have to experience eternal death, but rather eternal life.

'He loves you just as much as He loves me,' Enshi told them. 'And He wants you to experience that same freedom.'

For a moment Enshi thought he saw a glimmer of interest in the men's eyes. They wanted to believe him, he knew, but they realised how much it would cost them. And they weren't prepared to pay the price. Enshi knew that God had allowed him to present a simple Gospel message to men who probably had never heard it before. And he also knew that was the real reason he was locked in this prison. How else would these men hear the good news that could set them free?

As Enshi was silently thanking God for the opportunity He had just given him, another group of men – even angrier than those he already faced – stormed into the room. They towered over Enshi with looks on their faces that said they relished what they were about to do. Enshi knew these men. They were fellow prisoners who had agreed to collaborate with the prison leaders in exchange for privileges. Technically this was against the law, but in practice it was all too common.

As Enshi predicted, his 'stubbornness' did cost him. The beating the men gave him seemed particularly brutal, yet in spite of the pain that made tears stream down Enshi's cheeks, God once again gave him the grace to forgive those who were causing it. It would not make any sense, he knew, to share a message of God's love while hating those who had not yet accepted it.

Word about Enshi's beating swept quickly through the prison factory as everyone learned how this fearless man had stood up for his Christian beliefs. What could possibly be so important, they wondered, that someone would endure such humiliation and pain? One by one, men began to seek out Enshi to find the answer to that question. From highly educated professors and scholars who had been imprisoned as enemies of communism, to common criminals who had murdered friends in exchange for a few yuan – they came and asked Enshi about this Jesus.

'If your Jesus is really God,' they wanted to know, 'why won't He protect you from beatings? If He really set you free like you said, why are you still locked in this prison?'

Enshi answered them with an old Chinese idiom: *Zhen jin bu pa huo lian*. 'Real gold fears no fire,' he told them. 'We have to go through times of testing – the fire – but it's to find out what we're made of. If we ask Him, He'll be right there with us and we won't be burned. We won't even be singed. Instead we'll come out shining, purer than when we went in.'

Some believed. Others didn't. Some were willing to pay the price. Others weren't. Enshi smiled to himself as he realised that the communist government thought that hard labour, re-education and other man-inspired remedies were the answers to changing the hearts of criminals – indeed the hearts of all men. But as he watched even hardened murderers and thieves soften when they believed his message, he knew only the blood of Jesus could accomplish that seemingly impossible task.

Chapter 7

Torture and Persecution

*'He was oppressed and He was afflicted, yet He opened
not His mouth; He was led as a lamb to the slaughter,
and as a sheep before its shearers is silent, so He opened
not his mouth.'*   (Isaiah 53:7, NASB)

Enshi shifted his weight and tried not to think about the
searing pain that burned through every cell in his body. He
wanted to rub his sore arms and shoulders, but the cords
that so tightly held his hands together behind his back
would not allow that. It seemed to Enshi as if he had been
standing in the same spot for hours – and he probably had.
He had long ago lost track of what time or even what day it
was.

For the hundredth time, he tried to block out the ques-
tions being shouted at him by the men circled around him.
And for the thousandth time he prayed, 'God, give me
Your grace to endure this ... and have mercy on me.'

'What are you planning?' one man in the circle yelled at
him. 'Why do you hate communism so much?'

'What do "brother" and "sister" mean?' mocked
another, using curse words that made Enshi wince. 'It's so
phoney, all this talk about brothers and sisters! Why don't
you stop it?'

The questions, threats, mocking and curses continued in
a seemingly endless barrage, one after the other, on and on

and on. They were all part of *pidou*, a form of psychological persecution designed to wear down the accused.

The most difficult part was that *pidou* was conducted by fellow prisoners. In the government's quest to rid the country of dissent, anyone – even prisoners – was allowed to turn in someone else. On the flimsiest of accusations, someone could be forced to endure round after round of *pidou*. Sometimes that meant standing in the same spot for hours at a time, day after day, while others formed a circle shouting questions, lies and accusations. No matter what one said, it could quickly be twisted and used as grounds for further accusations. *Pidou* was a no-win situation.

Needless to say, Christians were not spared, and in fact seemed to be a favourite target. Prison authorities watched them and knew how well organised they were. They knew they had their own doctrines, their own teaching, and even their own book – the Bible. They were convinced that Christians were plotting a rebellion against the communist party. 'Cult' and 'counter-revolutionary' were just some of the names that they used to accuse and persecute Christians.

Those who did not know the Lord and could not call on Him for strength during *pidou* would collapse from the constant grilling and the pressure of questions shouted at full volume by people slamming their fists and pounding the table. Those who had never experienced *pidou* had no idea how they would react to such intense psychological intimidation. For some, their mouths would become dry and they would feel completely weak. Others would find their emotions jumbled and tossed about like a roller coaster – up one moment, down the next. Still others would succumb to the tremendous loss of dignity that *pidou* generated. Most people felt a combination of all three – and more. *Pidou* was psychological and mental torture at its worst.

Often, physical torture was added to compound the effects. In one of the cruellest forms of *pidou*, guards would force the hands of the accused behind his or her back and tie them with a rope that could then be used to violently jerk the hands up, thereby putting pressure on the shoulders and arm sockets. Cell mates standing around the circle would tighten the rope so that the knot would fly up and pull the person's hands with it, in some cases dislocating the shoulders from their sockets.

An even more vicious form of *pidou* was called 'riding a plane'. In addition to the rope tied around a person's arms and hands, a bamboo stick was inserted between the arm and rope. As *pidou* intensified – and if the answers given were not acceptable – someone would twist the stick and pull it higher and higher, causing excruciating pain to the shoulders.

Still other forms of *pidou* were designed to humiliate and belittle prisoners. Sometimes Enshi was outfitted in a tall, pointed 'dunce' hat with an enormous sign detailing his 'crimes'. Wearing this demeaning attire, he was forced to walk the streets while on-lookers jeered and joined the guards and others who hurled insults at him.

Pidou was mob psychology at its lowest form, carefully crafted to wear down the accused and force him to 'confess' to crimes he had never committed. And for many, it worked. Day after day of lies, accusations, and denunciations were more than some could take, and often Enshi would learn that a prisoner in a neighbouring cell had committed suicide rather than endure any more *pidou*. The torment and abuse were simply too much. One man electrocuted himself: another jumped off a smokestack to his death.

Yet for believers like Enshi, even the most extreme forms of *pidou* could not quench the fire that burned inside them. In spite of the almost unbearable physical pain and the degrading humiliation they were subjected to, there was such a sense of joy that the thought of suicide never occurred to them, even at times when *pidou* was at the most intense levels. Enshi could always count on receiving this help from above when he remembered the Scriptures he had memorised as a child – as well as the words to one of his favourite hymns, *God's Way*,

God's way is the best way, tho' I may not see
Why sorrows and trials oft gather 'round me.
He is ever seeking my gold to refine,
So humbly I trust Him, My Saviour divine.

God's way is the best way, God's way is the right
way,
I'll trust in Him alway, He knoweth the best.

God's way is the best way, my path He hath planned,
I'll trust in Him alway while holding His hand.
In shadow or sunshine He ever is near,
With Him for my refuge, I never need fear.

God's way is the best way, God's way is the right
way,
I'll trust in Him alway, He knoweth the best.

God's way shall be my way, He knoweth the best,
And leaning upon Him, sweet, sweet is my rest.
No harm can befall me, safe, safe shall I be,
I'll cling to Him ever, so precious is He.

God's way is the best way, God's way is the right
way,
I'll trust in Him alway, He knoweth the best.*

The believers' joy did not escape the notice of the guards, who taunted them more than ever and found excuses to *pidou* them whenever possible – always looking for some small crack in what they considered a carefully crafted facade. Often the guards would enlist the help of other prisoners by encouraging them to uncover (or if necessary invent) 'problem' areas and weak points among the believers.

Sometimes the more compassionate prisoners would feel

---

* *God's Way* by Lida Shivers Leech.

sorry for the believers. Christians, they knew, were living lives above reproach even under the most degrading circumstances and rarely if ever could they find an area to accuse them. But it was impossible to refuse orders, and they were forced to find something, however superficial. When it came time for these prisoners to *pidou* the Christians, Enshi always noticed that they tied his hands as loosely as possible and that the questions were not nearly as intense or venomous as those that others shouted. Silently, Enshi would always thank God for sending such mercy and would ask the Lord to bless these men in return for being a blessing to him.

And whenever possible Enshi would look for opportunities to share his faith – even during times of severe *pidou*.

'Why do you believe in Jesus?' someone would shout at him from the edge of the circle. 'What does this ridiculous term "Christian" mean? Are you some kind of a cult?'

Enshi would smile to himself as he realised this was the opportunity he was waiting for. Once again God had given him an opening to evangelise – even in the midst of imprisonment. Like Peter, Stephen and Paul, he would answer their questions by boldly proclaiming his faith.

'We are not members of a cult,' he would reply, 'but members of God's family. We follow Jesus Christ, and that's why we call ourselves Christians. Our Father in heaven sent His Son to die in our place, and we're His brothers and sisters.'

He explained that the terms 'brothers and sisters' were more than just words, that even in prison they felt an overwhelming sense of family with each other. 'We're not *trying* to be close,' he said in answer to their accusations. 'We *are* close. It's a fact. Because of Jesus, we're brothers and sisters.'

Enshi knew it was only a matter of time before the prison guards realised what he was doing, and invariably someone would stop him, putting an end to that round of *pidou* – at least for a while. Often he was ordered to be silent and sent to a locked room where he was told to write his 'confession' with paper and pen. The epistle-like documents that he turned in were filled with the Gospel message so that even the prison authorities who read them, looking for some sign of 'repentance', heard about Jesus and what He meant to the believers behind bars.

As severe as the *pidou* was that the men experienced, in the women's prison it was even more intense. Often, stories of what the women believers endured made their way back to Enshi and the others in the men's prison, who would pray for their sisters asking God to give them strength to endure – and opportunities to share their faith. One particular woman, Zhou Meilan, had been arrested along with twenty other believers at a house church that she had organised. As leader of the church, Zhou Meilan was charged with using religion to turn others against the government, and she was given a five-year prison sentence so that she could be re-educated and rehabilitated.

Well into her fifties, Zhou Meilan had neglected her own health during her years of serving others for the Lord, so she was already in an extremely weakened condition when she was imprisioned. Still she joyfully served the other women in her cell.

The guards, however, were not moved by her infirmity, and whipped and tortured her all the more violently. Because of the persecution, along with the harsh conditions in the prison, she soon caught tuberculosis. Finally her health weakened to the point that she was coughing up blood and was too weak even to get out of bed in the morning. Reluctantly the guards sent her to the prison clinic, and even there, she continually testified and shared the Lord with others, including several murderers who repented and accepted the love of Jesus into their hearts.

The non-Christian cell mates to whom she had shown so much kindness cared for her while she was sick – which made the prison officials all the angrier. They accused her of exerting undue influence upon others and manipulating them for her own benefit. Finally when their taunts failed to stop her, they decided it was time to *pidou* her. They rounded up her cell mates who wanted nothing to do with the guards' plans but they had no choice.

On a bitter cold winter day, her *pidou* began. Day after day she endured accusations, mocking, lies and curses, always with a dignity and strength that even some of the unbelievers in the room knew had to come from the God whom she so bravely defended. Finally after a week of such brutality, late one night she could not take it any more and she collapsed under the pressure, unconscious on the floor.

'You're just faking it,' the disgusted guards yelled at her, and took her limp body and threw it outside on to the ground that was frozen solid in the sub-zero weather.

No one else was allowed to go outside, and the rest of the meeting continued into the late hours of the night. Finally when the last denunciation had been uttered, the guards went outside to check on Zhou Meilan, but it was too late. She was dead.

The other Christian women in the prison asked for her body and permission to bury it, but the officials refused. The women knew that the guards were afraid that a rebellion would start, and they reluctantly went back to their quarters, weeping over the death of their sister. Somehow later that night, a few of the believers were able to secretly go outside to the spot where their precious sister lay. Although they would not be able to take her body or give her a decent burial, at least they would be able to see her for one last time on this side of heaven. Finally they spotted her body on the frozen, frost-covered ground. There Zhou Meilan lay dead – and on her face was a smile.

The testimony of her strong and determined faith spread not only throughout the women's prison but also to the men's prison. She had been so weak, they all knew, yet she endured until the end, even through such a violent and degrading death. The Lord had sustained her, even through *pidou*.

Chapter 8

Unity of the Brethren

'Behold, how good and how pleasant it is for brethren to dwell together in unity!' (Psalm 133:1)

For most Christians who were imprisoned during the Cultural Revolution in China, the most difficult part of their ordeal was not the torture. Nor was it the harsh conditions or the lack of food. It was not the disease that raced through the filthy cells, or the rats that gnawed on the few possessions they had. It was not even the cruel prison guards or the unending routine of days stretching one after the other without end.

For Christians who before their imprisonment were used to the encouragement of fellow believers, no matter how secretly they had to meet, the most difficult part of prison was that it was next to impossible to spend time with other believers – even if there were any other believers nearby. Yet God was faithful to bring brothers and sisters together and provide them with fellowship and encouragement, often in the most unexpected and miraculous ways.

Once, for example, Enshi was working in a factory where there were only four believers out of 1,000 men. Enshi had heard reports that there was a believer in a nearby prison, a man named Su Chingshan who had worked in a high government position where no one knew he was a believer. Su Chingshan, in fact, was a secret member of a house church in Beijing led by Wang Mingdao. Throughout the Christian church in China, Wang Mingdao was one of the best-known leaders of the underground house church movement. He had fearlessly refused to register his church with the government, and was himself now paying the penalty for his faith. When Wang was arrested, Su Chingshan was among those who were likewise thrown into prison.

Enshi and the other three brothers who worked in the prison factory were ecstatic to learn that Su Chingshan might be just a short distance from them. Stories of his joyful service to the Lord had quietly reached them, and the more they thought about it, the more they wanted to see this fellow prisoner. What an encouragement Su Chingshan would be to them, and they just might be able to encourage him. But how would they ever find him, they wondered? And even if they did, what chance would they have to make contact and share a word of encouragement – however briefly?

One day when the men heard that Su Chingshan had been relocated to a work farm even closer to their factory, they decided that the time was right. Enshi, they knew, had more freedom than any of them and was often allowed out of the factory on work assignments. They talked it over, prayed about it, and Enshi agreed to try to contact Su Chingshan. How he was going to do that, however, he hadn't the foggiest idea – especially because he had never met Su Chingshan and there was no one to tell him what he looked like. It didn't seem as if there was any human way to make contact, so Enshi and the other brothers waited for the Lord to show them how to do it.

One afternoon a prison official called Enshi to his office and gave him an assignment that would take him outside the factory walls. As soon as Enshi left the official's quarters, he found the other brothers and told them this was the opportunity they had prayed for. Under their breaths, they each whispered the same prayer – that God would guide Enshi and sovereignly show him how to recognise Su Chingshan. None of the men wanted to voice their fears, but they knew if Enshi made one false move, there would be trouble – for them and for Su Chingshan. The only way to avoid that was to rely completely on God's timing.

Enshi set out on his mission, praying as each step moved him further from the factory – and hopefully closer to Su Chingshan. His route took him down dusty village lanes as he breathed in the free air and relished the sight of children playing with bamboo sticks, women washing out rags in chipped enamel bowls and sweeping the ever-present dust from cobblestones on the streets. Even the mundane everyday activities of this quiet village seemed precious to a man who had been held prisoner for so many years. Occasionally he would see a young woman who would remind him of Huiliang, and wistfully he would long for the sight of her face and the encouraging word she invariably spoke. For all he knew, she had probably married someone else. Why would someone as special as Huiliang wait around for him when there were plenty of other men asking to marry her?

But Enshi knew it was senseless to think about Huiliang and whether or not she had married someone else. As quickly as the thoughts of her entered his mind, he pushed them out. Instead, Enshi stopped to talk with a group of children and casually looked behind him. There was always the possibility, he knew, that he would be followed, and he did not want to risk endangering Su Chingshan for a few moments of fellowship. As far as he could tell, however, there was no one trailing him. Besides the children, the only other inhabitants of the street were a few mangy chickens that would soon be someone's dinner.

Leaving the chickens and the children behind, Enshi casually moved on, at each intersection choosing the route that took him closer to the edge of town. Finally the rice fields were in view. Enshi took one more glance behind him and when he was sure he wasn't being followed, left the village altogether and headed for the fields. If Su Chingshan was working on a farm, Enshi knew this would be the logical place to look for him. But all he could see was acre after acre of rice fields stretching as far as his eye could see. Su Chingshan could be anywhere.

He wouldn't find him by standing in one spot, he told himself, and he'd look less obvious if he kept moving. The rows between rice paddies served as walkways. Enshi chose one and began walking down it. Here and there he saw people working, and whenever he passed someone, he would quickly look the man over, then lower his head and quietly mutter a greeting.

Far ahead of him, Enshi heard voices and spotted a long line of workers carrying baskets of rice. They were walking single file on the path between rice paddies, and although Enshi couldn't make out what they were saying, he guessed by the tone of the voices that these must be guards shouting orders to prisoners.

Enshi knew the men weren't from his own prison and therefore they had to be from Su Chingshan's. Somewhere in the group was the brother he was looking for – but where? There must have been 200 men in the long line snaking through the paddy. It was out of the question to ask someone to direct him to Su Chingshan because it would only draw attention to both of them. Enshi knew the only possibility of finding Su Chingshan in such a crowd was for the Lord to point him out.

Suddenly Enshi's eyes were drawn to one man. It was as if God had shot an arrow straight from heaven to aim his attention at this one particular man in the midst of all the others. Even more surprising was the fact that the man was not in the long line of prisoners but rather sitting down, resting, and fanning himself with a straw hat. Why would a prisoner be sitting down, Enshi asked himself, but he was positive the Lord was telling him to talk with this man. Taking a deep breath and praying silently, Enshi tried to look as casual as possible as he walked over to him. Since he could think of nothing else to say, he simply stated exactly what was on his mind.

'Do you know Su Chingshan?' he asked bluntly.

The man stared at Enshi for a few moments, then he said, 'Why do you need to find him?'

'Someone asked me to come here and identify him,' Enshi replied.

The man stopped fanning himself and put down his hat. He looked Enshi straight in the eye and said, 'I am he.'

Enshi almost felt weak as he realised that out of 200 men in the field, the Holy Spirit had directed him to exactly whom he was looking for. A bolt of joy surged through him, and the instantaneous sense of oneness, unity and brotherhood he felt with his new-found brother was almost overwhelming. Su Chingshan, too, must have sensed the same emotions, for his face showed that he, too, knew he had found a brother.

Enshi wiped the tears from his eyes as the pressure of the long prison sentence was relieved, however momentarily, by the joy of such sweet fellowship. He knew that Su Chingshan's response – 'I am he' – referred to the account in the Bible of Moses' face-to-face encounter with God. When Moses asked God what His name was, He replied, *'I AM who I AM'* (Exodus 3:14). Because Su Chingshan gave a similar response, Enshi knew that he was telling him they both believed in the same God, and even though they had never set eyes on each other before, they were brothers. The bond between them was unbreakable – the same sweet encouragement and fellowship that had enabled saints through the ages to persevere. Humbly Enshi realised God loved them both so much that He had taken a moment out of running the universe to arrange this special encounter.

There was so much to say, yet both men knew that any moment the guards could break up their meeting. Enshi quickly told Su Chingshan that there were other brothers nearby who sent their greetings and love.

'Do you have any urgent needs that we can pray about for you?' he asked.

'No, nothing at all,' Su Chingshan replied, smiling. Enshi realised for Su Chingshan, too, this encounter was all he needed to get through another week – or another year, if necessary. How could he ask for anything more from a God who had already taken care of him so faithfully and provided answers to prayers he hadn't even voiced?

Chapter 9

'Do You Have Some Secret?'

'Consider it all joy, my brethren, when you encounter various trials, knowing that the testing of your faith produces endurance. And let endurance have its perfect result, that you may be perfect and complete, lacking in nothing.'
(James 1:2–4, NASB)

Enshi adjusted the load of bamboo that pressed deep into his back and shoulders. There was one particular pole among the dozens he carried that seemed to be aimed right at the centre of his left shoulder blade. With every step he took down the slippery mountain path, the pole gnawed deeper into his skin. Enshi knew when he finally got back to the prison many hours later that his shirt would be caked with blood.

Another blister, he sighed to himself. He prayed that this one wouldn't get infected as the others had.

More than anything, Enshi wanted to stop just for a few precious minutes to readjust the weight of the bamboo on his back, but he knew that even a short break might make him late. It wasn't worth three minutes now to endure the beating he would get later if he wasn't on time returning to the prison camp.

After so many times hiking up this same path and gingerly walking down it again, Enshi had memorised every centimetre of it. In a few moments he'd reach the next 'landmark' – a sharp bend to the right that told him in another twenty minutes he would be on level ground. There he could remove the load of bamboo from his back once and for all – at least until tomorrow when the entire process would start all over again.

Just before Enshi reached the bend, however, he came to an abrupt halt. There in the middle of the path right in front of him lay a man whom Enshi recognised as Jin Weili, a prisoner from another cell block to whom he had spoken only in passing. Quickly Enshi pulled him to his feet and helped him gather the bamboo poles that had scattered in every direction.

'We'd better hurry,' Enshi told him, but Jin Weili looked as if the last thing he wanted to do was carry the heavy load even a step further. Instead he told Enshi that he wanted to leave the poles right where they had fallen and make a run for it into the woods. But Enshi quickly talked him out of his hastily concocted plan, reminding him of the miserable success rate of other prisoners who had tried to escape.

Reluctantly Jin Weili agreed with him, heaved the bamboo load onto his back, and began to follow Enshi down the mountain. Since the poles jutted out on either side of the men, they could not walk side by side on the narrow path, but instead walked one behind the other with Enshi leading the way. Jin Weili stared at the man in front of him whose steps seemed to be a hundred times more energetic than his own.

'How can you put up with this?' he asked. 'And how come you're always smiling and singing? Do you have some secret that I don't know about?'

Enshi laughed out loud. 'Yes, I do, as a matter of fact,' he said, turning his head so that Jin Weili could hear him. 'My secret is Jesus. As long as I keep my eyes on Him instead of the circumstances, it doesn't matter what goes on around me. My joy depends on Him, not on the circumstances.'

'That's fine for you,' Jin Weili replied, 'but it wouldn't work for me. The only thing that will make me happy is getting out of this place.'

'Just because you're released from prison doesn't make you free,' Enshi said. 'True freedom is a freedom that no man in this world can give. The Bible says, *"You shall know the truth and the truth shall make you free ... Therefore if the Son makes you free, you are free indeed"'* (John 8:32, 36).

Enshi went on to tell Jin Weili that this was more than just a philosophy or an escape mechanism to get him through the difficult times. It was a heavenly exchange: if Enshi reached out to God, God would give him the strength he needed to get through each day – and do it with joy.

Jin Weili had to admit he was intrigued by what Enshi told him. The harsh work in the labour camp often stretched past fifteen hours a day, followed by hours of indoctrination meetings where communist cadres droned on about Marxist philosophy. In the face of the endless days and nights, Jin Weili had worked out his own way to cope – anger, hate and weeks of deep, seemingly bottomless depression.

Yet he never failed to be amazed by the reaction of Enshi and the other believers. They were going through exactly the same circumstances as he was – worse, actually, because they were persecuted even more severely for being Christians. He was just an 'intellectual' who was in prison supposedly for crimes against the state. Yet the reaction of the believers was completely different. The more trying the circumstances, the more joy seemed to radiate from their faces.

'Look,' Enshi told him, 'if you don't believe me, let me tell you about someone in the women's prison on the other side of town. She's a believer just like me.'

Enshi explained that Wang Lipin was already in her late fifties when she and her husband – both full-time servants of the Lord – were arrested for preaching the Gospel in the deep mountainous regions of China. Raised in a big city, she knew nothing about farms or what it took to survive in rural areas. Yet when she was assigned to heavy labour in a

71

factory out in the country, even carrying 150 pounds of coal in baskets at the end of bamboo poles didn't lessen her joy.

In fact, in spite of her age, prison officials actually used Wang Lipin as an example to challenge younger workers. She never missed an opportunity to say it was God's grace that enabled her to work hard, and her joy was a tremendous encouragement to others – both believers and non-believers alike.

Of course, Enshi continued, she was not always on the good side of the officials, and their attempts to re-educate her and destroy her Christian beliefs continued unabated. But she never failed to testify about the Lord, even in times of persecution. When she was asked to write her confession, for example, she would spend the time singing hymns and songs of praise. When she was mercilessly persecuted and forced to endure the most intense *pidou*, her face radiated joy. And when others were the object of *pidou*, she would lovingly care for them when they returned to their cells, encouraging them with Scriptures and songs.

She never spoke against the officials, but instead encouraged others to love their enemies. When she told people that she regularly prayed for Chairman Mao, China's leader, who was responsible for their prison sentences, they were shocked. But she told them he was a sinner and needed salvation just like everyone else – and that is what she was praying for.

In her desire to serve others, Wang Lipin never complained about her own circumstances – and there was plenty she could have complained about. Instead of supporting her Christian stance, both her daughter and son had renounced her, the police had ransacked her home, and she constantly received reports that her beloved husband, who was also in prison, was being persecuted unmercifully for his faith and work as a minister.

Yet no matter how bad circumstances got, her joy and boldness never wavered. Her voice could be heard throughout the prison night and day praying and singing hymns of praise to encourage the others. Her favourite hymn was *Heaven Is My Home*, which she sang over and over again,

Heaven is my home.
Earth is a desert drear.
Heaven is my home.
Danger and sorrow stand
Round me on every hand.
Heaven is my Fatherland.
Heaven is my home.*

For Wang Lipin, those words were true. Although her body was locked in a prison, her spirit lived in His presence. Even unbelievers would look at her and say, 'There is someone who doesn't know the worries of this world. It's almost as if she lives in heaven.'

They began to call her 'the lady with joy' and the 'citizen of heaven'. Many who saw her believed in Jesus as a result of her joy – including prison guards. Finally after many years in prison and labour camps, Wang Lipin received word that her husband had died in prison. There were hushed reports that his body was covered with bruises when it was found, leading Wang Lipin and the others to conclude that he had been tortured and beaten to death. Yet even in the face of this devastating news, Wang Lipin praised God because she realised He had prepared her for her husband's death with the words to the song she sang night and day.

The officials who broke the news to her were appalled by her reaction. She laughed out loud telling them she was delighted that her husband had gone to heaven, the 'highest place'. The officials were doubly disturbed by her reaction because they were hoping she would break down in tears – an offence that was punishable by whipping. But for Wang Lipin, the words to her favourite song were a reality for her husband.

Years later, Wang Lipin's time came also. The harsh prison life had finally taken a toll on her frail body, and she

---

* *Heaven Is My Home* by Thomas R. Taylor and Lowell Mason.

knew her strength was almost gone. She gathered her beloved sisters together to share with them one final time.

'Love your enemies and pray for them,' she told them with a voice so weakened by malnutrition, back-breaking work and intense persecution that it was barely a whisper. 'Nothing is empty when you pray. And remember not to worry about what will happen to you. Worries do not add a single benefit to you.'

An hour later, heaven did become home for Wang Lipin. She was undoubtedly greeted there by others who had believed in Jesus because of her joy.

Enshi finished his story just as he and Jin Weili reached the others who had brought their cargo of bamboo from all parts of the mountain. As Enshi rubbed his aching shoulders, he thanked God for another opportunity to share Christ's ways with a fellow prisoner. The message he had given Jin Weili was completely contrary to what Jin Weili had grown up with, and only by revelation would Jin Weili understand the difference between happiness and joy. Happiness is determined by circumstances, Enshi knew, but joy comes from God, requiring that we walk closely with Him no matter what the circumstances.

With prison guards all around them now, Enshi and Jin Weili could not continue their discussion, but the rest of the way home Enshi prayed that Jin Weili would understand what he had told him, and that he, too, would make a decision to follow the One from whom joy flows.

Chapter 10

Escape From Death

'Though I walk through the valley of the shadow of death, I will fear no evil; for You are with me.'
(Psalm 23:4)

Enshi was exhausted and hungry beyond anything he had ever felt before. It was only 2:00 in the afternoon and he still had hours of back-breaking work ahead of him before he was back in camp. And even then he would not be able to collapse on his flea-infested cot because he would still have to endure an evening's worth of lectures on the glories of socialism and the wisdom of Chairman Mao.

The hunger pangs tearing at his stomach threatened to gnaw right through his body. He scoured the woods hoping to find something – anything – that would fill his empty insides. He *had* to have something to eat, he told himself, and he had to have it *now*. Suddenly out of the corner of his eye he spotted something poking out of the ground. Wild mushrooms! There was one little cluster of them – like a miniature forest of trees just waiting for him to chop down and devour.

Yet in spite of Enshi's joy at finding this meal all prepared for him – and in spite of the pangs in his stomach that were calling for him to send some food their way – Enshi knew that picking wild mushrooms could be a dangerous proposition. There were plenty of varieties of edible mushrooms that could make a tasty meal, but many other varieties could cause extreme sickness or even death. Enshi had learned a little about mushrooms during his time in prison, but this variety was one he had never seen before. Were they safe ... or would he be sorry he ate them?

Finally his intense hunger caused every rational thought to fly right out of his head. Enshi said a quick prayer asking God to protect him, and without even taking time to clean the mushrooms, he quickly snapped them from their delicate bases and popped them into his mouth. It wasn't long before he was sorry he had done it. Suddenly the hunger pangs were dwarfed by much stronger pains that Enshi knew could only come from one source. The mushrooms must have been an inedible variety. He only hoped they weren't fatal.

Enshi was hours away from another human being, not to mention the prison camp and hospital, so there was nothing he could do – nothing that is, but ask the Lord to counteract any poison he might have consumed. But the pain only grew worse, and in Enshi's already weak state of health, he didn't know how long he could hold on. Still, he knew he had to gather his required allotment of roots, or he would receive a beating that would make the pain he was feeling at the moment feel like nothing but a small bruise. And so to keep his mind off the pain, he kept working, trying to gather roots and work his way down the mountain.

Just as he was prying a particularly deep root loose from the packed soil, he heard someone calling him from a nearby grove of trees. Enshi was elated to find the voice belonged to Jin Zhongsheng, a fellow believer. Quickly Enshi explained what had happened, and Jin Zhongsheng immediately began gathering herbs, which he insisted Enshi eat. Jin Zhongsheng did not tell his friend that he didn't really know if the herbs would help, but he was desperate for anything that might counteract the poison and save his friend's life.

It was a long day as Enshi and Jin Zhongsheng worked, praying whenever they could that God would do a miracle. By the time they returned to the camp, they knew God had answered their prayers. The pains in Enshi's stomach were completely gone. Enshi never knew if the mushrooms he had eaten were in fact poisonous or just upsetting to his system, but he did know that God answered his prayers because he was completely healed.

It was not the first time that the Lord had saved his life while he was in prison. It seemed as if the devil was not satisfied that Enshi was behind bars; he wanted him dead – and would stop at nothing to achieve that goal. Enshi remembered a time when he was gathering bamboo. God not only helped Enshi find enough bamboo each day to fulfil the 100-pound-per-prisoner requirement, but he also showed him how to bind the heavy stalks in order to keep them from coming untied on the way down the mountain.

One rainy afternoon Enshi was manoeuvring down a steep slope carrying his unwieldy load. He tried to ignore the rocky cliff on his right that plunged to the valley far below. Instead he kept his focus on the slippery path – made even more treacherous by the constant rain. Heavy storms, he knew, would quickly wash away the mud, but today the rain was slow and steady, and the path was awash with slippery mud, hidden rocks, and other unseen hazards. One false move and he would be down the mountainside a lot quicker than he intended.

Without warning, the left tip of the pole he was carrying caught on the side of the mountain, throwing him completely off balance. Normally he would have been able to catch himself, but because of the rain, he tumbled over the side of the cliff and rapidly started falling toward the valley below. Enshi knew there was nothing between him and it, and unless God intervened, he was a dead man.

Suddenly, he felt himself being abruptly jerked to a halt. Enshi looked up to see what had happened, and realised the two ends of the pole he was carrying had caught on trees, completely stopping his fall. If only one side had caught, he realised, he would have continued to fall. What were the chances, he wondered, of the pole catching on two trees on either side at the exact same moment? It wasn't just coincidence, he knew; it was providence. God had once again saved his life.

Time and again Enshi saw the hand of God save him when others were killed. When he worked in the sugarcane factory with dangerous machines all around, God saved him when his coat caught on a blade and threatened to suck him into the whirling machine. When a high fever threatened to take his life and there was no medicine to heal him, God used a simple bowl of rice – the only food available – to bring down his temperature and restore him to health.

But it was when guards ransacked his belongings looking for what they considered contraband that Enshi appreciated God's sovereign protection the most. The guards knew Enshi was a Christian and although Bibles were absolutely forbidden in prison, they suspected he had one. In fact, Enshi did have a Bible, and it was his most precious possession. It was not a complete Bible – only a tiny pocket-size edition of the four Gospels – but it was a lot more than most believers had.

By nothing short of a miracle, Enshi had managed to sneak this copy of the Scriptures into prison when he was first arrested. Other believers had to rely on friends and family members to bring them a single page at a time whenever they came to the prison on visits. They would tear pages from their own Bibles – assuming they even had a copy – and hide them in something they brought for the prisoners. Once inside the prison walls, the single page would be passed from hand to hand where it was read until each verse was virtually memorised. The prisoners never knew when they would see the page again.

Bibles were precious commodities in prison, and Enshi prayed every day that God would protect his small book from anything or anyone who would try to take it away. It was impossible to read Scriptures openly, of course, so Enshi would wait until late at night while everyone else was asleep. Fortunately, the guards left the lights on all night, fearing that prisoners would escape. That made it easier for Enshi to read underneath his mosquito netting, but it also made it easier to be spotted doing something that was against the rules. The danger was enormous because guards would reward prisoners for turning in their cellmates, so Enshi lived with the constant fear that even if a guard didn't spot him, another prisoner would.

Night after night, Enshi risked discovery and read the Gospels until he couldn't keep his eyes open any longer. Then he would pray and ask the Holy Spirit to show him where to hide his precious book. His task complete, he closed his eyes and prepared for what would happen when he woke up. And sure enough, the same scene would be repeated every morning. Like clockwork the guards would go from cell to cell on their relentless search to find something that could be another excuse to beat the prisoners.

But day after day, God protected Enshi and his copy of the Gospels. If he hid it in his pillow, the guards would tear apart his blanket. If it was hiding in the wall behind a loose stone, the guard would rip open his pillow. If Enshi had wrapped it at the foot of his blanket, they went through his clothes.

Week after week, month after month, year after year, the searches went on – and the guards never did find Enshi's hidden treasure in all the time he was in prison.

Chapter 11

To the Uttermost Parts of China

'The kings of the earth set themselves, and the rulers take counsel together against the Lord and against His Anointed ... He who sits in the heavens shall laugh.'
(Psalm 2:2, 4)

'Pssst!'

Enshi tried to ignore the man calling to him in the dark. 'Pssst! You there! I need to talk with you!'

The voice, Enshi knew, was that of a prisoner named Fang Heli, one of many wedged into the tiny cell next to Enshi's. Enshi looked around the barracks to make sure no one had heard the man call him. It was late at night and all prisoners were supposed to be in bed and quiet. If soldiers saw them talking, there would be trouble to pay.

Enshi tried to ignore the persistent questioning, but Fang Heli would not let up, 'You're a believer, aren't you, Enshi?'

Enshi paused, praying that no one would hear his response. 'I am,' he quietly replied.

'Then I must talk to you – now. I heard people talking about a man named Jesus, and I need to know who He is. Can you tell me?'

Enshi sighed to himself. This was the kind of opportunity he prayed for in prison, but he knew this was not the time to answer Fang Heli's questions. If they were caught talking, it wouldn't benefit either of them. 'Go back to sleep,' he told Fang Heli. 'I'll talk to you tomorrow and explain everything.'

The next morning as soon as Enshi was up and dressed, he looked for Fang Heli, but he was already gone. Enshi searched the line of men waiting to receive the watered-down rice that the guards were handing out for breakfast, but Fang Heli was nowhere to be found. He looked for him as he made his way to the day's work assignment, but still there was no sign of him. As soon as Enshi found out where Fang Heli was, he planned to set aside time to talk with him and explain the road to salvation – a simple road, but one that many were not yet willing to take. Fang Heli, it seemed, was ready,

But as the day went on, Enshi seemed to run into everyone but Fang Heli. Late in the afternoon, he spotted another prisoner who he thought might know Fang Heli's whereabouts. As they were loading coal into bamboo baskets, Enshi slowly worked his way over to the man, waited for an opportune moment, and then quietly whispered his question. 'I'm looking for Fang Heli,' he said. 'Do you know where he is?'

'Fang Heli?' the man replied. 'Yes, I know where he is. He's dead.'

'Dead!' gasped Enshi. 'What do you mean? I saw him just last night. How can he be dead?'

'Very simple,' the man replied. 'He was in town this morning on an errand for the guards when he was hit by a car. Boom. It was over before he knew what got him.'

Enshi was stunned. How could this happen? Fang Heli had been so ready to accept the Gospel message. One after another, questions filled Enshi's mind as he realised the cost of his hesitancy. How could he let himself be intimidated and bullied by the guards and their ridiculous regulations? Why hadn't he talked to Fang Heli when he had the chance?

Enshi's hesitancy caused him weeks of remorse. The only good that came of Fang Heli's untimely death was Enshi's vow that he would never again miss an opportunity to share the Gospel – no matter what it might cost him. Even in prison, he knew, there was a certain 'comfort zone', and Enshi resolved not to stay there unless absolutely necessary. Never again, he promised himself, would he pass an opening to share God's love with those who were ready to receive it. If others were willing to lay down their lives to spread the Gospel, he told himself, he could do no less.

He thought about the students he knew who had come to his house church. They were truly willing to pay with their lives to spread the Gospel – and the Lord used their willingness in miraculous ways. Enshi remembered how many of the students came from good families where education was highly valued. These were young people who diligently worked night and day, going to class, studying and taking exams.

Many of them graduated with honours from their universities, yet as soon as the government found out they were attending unregistered house churches,* they branded them 'counter-revolutionaries'. The government was supposed to honour their requests for work assignments, but instead punished these young believers by assigning them to the worst possible jobs – often in rural areas of provinces far from their home towns. In spite of degrees or academic honours, they were forced to do menial labour.

High school students who were believers paid for their faith in the same degrading manner. No matter how high their grades, they were not permitted to attend college or university. Instead, they were assigned to heavy labour in remote provinces, far from friends and families. Yet God honoured the commitment of these high school and college students – not only by giving them grace to endure often humiliating circumstances, but also by allowing them to participate in a spiritual harvest of immense proportions. No Christians had ever visited the remote villages where

---

* For an explanation of China's house church movement, see Chapter 16.

the students were sent, and so when they arrived, the Gospel arrived with them.

Their boldness and determination to share their faith – however difficult the circumstances – meant that hundreds of Chinese in rural areas had an opportunity to hear the life-changing message of Jesus Christ. As a result, the Gospel spread rapidly from one small village to another, and the churches that formed are still operating today.

Enshi knew that the students' boldness could have cost them plenty had they been discovered. But the students saw the bigger picture: They knew they had been sent to these distant locations not just by an order from the government but also by a divine order of God. It was He who used their circumstances to spread the Gospel to people who otherwise would not have an opportunity to hear it.

Enshi laughed to himself when he thought about what a guard had told him just a few days earlier.

'You Christians are contagious – like a bad disease!' the man had angrily shouted. 'There's a smell on you, and no matter where you go people know you're Christians. It's like a force, an influence, and it's very contagious to others!'

Enshi knew the guard was using this as an excuse to isolate Christians, but he had to smile when he realised that even the guard – an avowed atheist and probably a communist party member – recognised the power of the Gospel to spread and touch people.

He remembered the story of a believer in a nearby women's prison. Even as a young child, Hua Meili could sing like an angel. But as the noose of repression tightened around the necks of China's Christians, it was Hua Meili's voice that got her into trouble. She told anyone who would listen that her voice was a gift from God. Even when she studied in music school, she refused to sing for 'show' or for money.

'My voice is not to entertain others,' she would steadfastly say, 'but to please God, to bless the brothers and sisters, and to do the work of the Lord.'

Finally one day her unwavering convictions came face to face with the school officials who were equally immovable in their atheistic beliefs. The headmaster of the school called Hua Meili to his office and announced that she had been chosen for a great honour: to represent the school and China by going to North Korea to sing for the Chinese soldiers fighting there. As important an honour as it was and as much as Hua Meili knew it would advance her career as a vocalist, she refused to go. Patiently she explained that such singing was against her principles and Christian beliefs. The dispute reached an impasse, and finally the headmaster had no choice but to expel Hua Meili from school.

Hua Meili returned to her hometown where she actively participated in her family's house church. Since she had already ignored the government's commands, she was branded a troublemaker and was carefully watched. It wasn't long before her 'illegal' church activities were discovered, and she was arrested and thrown into prison. The days turned into weeks, then months, and then years. Here, too, Hua Meili faced threats from government officials who found it a challenge to see if they could persuade her to back down.

One officer, for example, arranged for her to sing at an upcoming party, but as always, Hua Meili refused. The man was aghast that anyone would refuse his command and angrily removed his gun from its holster and pointed it directly at her head. And just to make sure she got the message, with his other hand he whipped out a knife and held it to her throat.

'Now you'll sing for the celebration,' he told her. 'If you don't, I'll cut off your head!'

In spite of the weapons held only inches from her face, Hua Meili did not flinch. 'I don't want to sing,' she replied. 'My voice is only for God, not for man.'

'Don't you realise the power I have over you? If you refuse to sing, I can kill you!'

'You want to kill me?' Hua Meili boldly answered. 'Go right ahead. I'm actually looking forward to seeing my Father in heaven. If it's God's will, I'm not afraid to die.'

The officer was seething, but he knew he had met his match. It wasn't worth killing her, so he backed down. But he became more determined than ever to coerce Hua Meili into doing what she did not want to do. More verbal threats followed and even physical abuse, but over and over again Hua Meili's reply was the same. Other officers also tried to break her will. They knew, for example, she had been born and bred in the city and consequently knew nothing about farm animals. So when it came time to assign oxen to the prisoners for their work in the fields, they made sure Hua Meili received the most stubborn, untrained animals available.

But Hua Meili refused to be swayed by their actions. She simply prayed, 'Lord, You know this animal is untrained and unruly. Please make him behave so I won't have any trouble working with him today.'

And to everyone's amazement, when she got her hands on the once recalcitrant beast, he actually behaved like an animal that had been through the most rigorous obedience training.

Hua Meili's commitment to God did not go unnoticed by the other prisoners – especially those who did not know anything about this God to whom she was so dedicated. One by one, they would seek her out – in the night, during the day at work assignments, wherever they could find a few moments to ask her about her faith. Many came to the Lord because of her strong example.

Enshi could only praise God when he realised no matter what devious plans the guards and officials would send the Christians' way, God was always victorious. In spite of the government's attempts to thwart the spread of Christianity, God's Kingdom was spreading throughout China – often through the very means sent to stop it.

Enshi thought again of the students, of Hua Meili and of others like them. He determined to be more faithful to the Lord and to their brothers and sisters in Christ. He asked God to help him never to miss the chance of telling anyone like Fang Heli the Good News of the Gospel.

Chapter 12

Protecting the Family

'I have been young, and now am old; yet I have not seen the righteous forsaken, nor his descendants begging bread.' (Psalm 37:25)

For Enshi, one of the most difficult parts of prison life was knowing that Huiliang and his parents were enduring their own persecution simply because of their relationship with him. Enshi had heard countless stories about how the government mercilessly punished family and friends of prisoners. No one, it seemed, could escape the intense paranoia that was sweeping through China.

If someone was imprisoned for being a 'counter-revolutionary', their parents, children, brothers, sisters and friends all suffered right along with them. It was almost impossible for friends and family members to find jobs – or keep the ones they already had. A negative mark in an employment file could shadow them for years and prevent them from ever obtaining gainful employment. Nobody, it seemed, could escape.

Friends and family were constantly faced with the agonising decision of remaining loyal to the imprisoned, or turning against them to insure their own safety. Huiliang constantly faced pressure from friends who urged her to renounce her friendship with Enshi.

In the face of such pressure, church members invariably

banded together to help those who were being persecuted. Enshi had heard about the family of a man who was imprisoned for 'illegal' religious activities. While the husband was in prison, his wife continued sharing the Gospel and holding meetings at home. It wasn't long before she, too, was arrested, leaving their two young children at home to fend for themselves with no food, money, or protection.

But the couple had been loyal church members, so the other believers in their house church took it upon themselves to care for the youngsters, always encouraging the children not to turn against their parents – in spite of government pressure to do so. They provided them with food and clothing, cooked for them, and prayed for them when government officials would come calling. Often the children would wake up to find that a bag of vegetables had been left on the doorstep overnight.

All these good works, Enshi knew, had to be done in secret because if the believers were discovered helping children of 'state enemies', there would have been trouble – not just for them, but for the children themselves. Receiving assistance from Christians was practically a crime in itself. Yet in spite of the danger, the secret aid continued for twenty years – the entire time that the couple were imprisoned. Finally the day came for their release, but the husband was so sick from the abuse he had suffered during his prison term that he died not long after his release. The wife was again left to care for herself and her children. And once again the believers came to their aid, providing for all their needs.

Enshi heard a similar story about another believer whose husband was in prison. Su Yinling was known for her boldness. Whether she was in a public place or at her job, she told everyone she was a Christian, not worrying about the consequences. Even when she developed both tuberculosis and other serious lung problems, her spiritual stamina only seemed to intensify. Of course, Su Yinling suffered deeply for her bold testimony. Over and over again, she was called for questioning and ordered to write confessions about herself and other believers.

'What kind of religious activities are you pursuing? Whom do you meet with? What is the name of the leader of this cult that you call a church?'

The grilling often continued for hours, and would let up only when Su Yinling was ordered to write out her confession on paper. Other times the police would not wait for her to show up at work in order to question her. They would come directly to her home and begin their harassment without warning. Day and night, around the clock, it seemed, the pounding and knocks would come on the door – and there was nothing Su Yinling could do but cooperate. She refused to give any information about other believers, but when it came to herself, she always told the truth – even when it got her into more trouble with the authorities.

The endless meetings, questions, and indoctrination sessions took their toll on Su Yinling's already frail health, and the doctors told her she needed complete bed rest for three months or they couldn't guarantee she would ever get well. Such a prescription was out of the question for someone who was married to a 'counter-revolutionary'. Instead Su Yinling was told she was being sent to a farm in a far-off mountain village where she would join other intellectuals who were being re-educated.

Su Yinling knew she was too weak to even walk, much less work on a farm. But what really discouraged her was the realisation that there was probably no chance of finding other believers on the farm. Su Yinling told herself that she welcomed the opportunity to share the Gospel with non-believers, but in her weakened condition, she also needed to have other Christians nearby who would pray for her and help her recover.

Over and over she prayed the words of Psalm 27,

> 'For in the time of trouble He shall hide me in His pavilion; in the secret place of His tabernacle He shall hide me; He shall set me high upon a rock ... I would

have lost heart, unless I had believed that I would see
the goodness of the Lord in the land of the living.'
(verses 5, 13)

Su Yinling arrived at the farm barely able to walk. She
was assigned a dirty bunk in one of the women's areas, and
was ordered to be at an indoctrination meeting in thirty
minutes when her re-education would begin. All Su Yinling
could do was sit on the bunk and repeat the same prayers
she had been saying for days. In the midst of her fervent
talk with the Lord, she heard a voice behind her,

'Excuse me, you must have just arrived. My name is Han
Liding.'

Su Yinling turned around to see who was talking to her,
and was shocked to find a familiar face. Han Liding was
none other than one of Su Yinling's old high school
teachers.

'Han Liding, what are you doing here?' Su Yinling said.

'Same as you,' Han Liding laughed. 'I'm being "re-
educated" to rid me of all those fancy beliefs in Jesus! But
praise God, I've been praying to Him to send me a fellow
Christian, and now He has. We're together again!'

As the two women talked, Su Yinling was further surprised to learn that in the years since they had seen each
other, Han Liding had become a medical doctor. Suddenly
she began to see God's plan for her, and in the weeks that
followed, Han Liding provided the care and attention that
Su Yinling's weak body needed so desperately. Everyday
she told her what to eat to accelerate her healing. Because
they were on a farm, they could eat much better rice than
was available in the city. They were even permitted to take
evening walks in the clean mountain air, which helped Su
Yinling's body grow stronger and stronger.

Su Yinling had to admit that, in spite of the gruelling
work, her stay on the farm was virtually like spending a
vacation in a mountain resort compared with what she had
to endure in the city.

In addition to the other intellectuals on the work farm,

there were students who were also required to undergo re-education. Many of them were young and had never been away from home on their own. Although Su Yinling was barely thirty years old herself, she knew she had to help the students survive or they would never make it. So she, Han Liding, and a few other Christian women decided to cook for the students, mend their clothes, and help them endure their re-education. In addition to physical help, they also provided spiritual help, and shared the Gospel with them whenever they could. As believers, they knew God had brought them to this place for a very special reason – to continue spreading His message throughout China.

Satan, of course, never gave up his mission. The more the believers rejoiced in the Lord, the more he tried to make them stop. One day the leader of the work farm told Su Yinling that she was being sent to a new assignment – to a remote mountain where her job would be to feed pigs. Since the location was so far away, she would have to live there by herself the entire time of her assignment.

Su Yinling had been born and bred in big cities and had never even fed a chicken, much less a herd of pigs who could easily crush her to death without anyone knowing. The thought of her new assignment was almost more than she could bear. 'I can't do it, Lord!' she cried. 'Please show me how to get out of this.'

Suddenly an idea came to her. The next morning Su Yinling went to see the wife of the farm leader. 'Mrs Wang,' she said, 'is there anyone among the ladies in the village who has ever been sent to the mountains to feed pigs?'

'Absolutely not,' Mrs Wang replied. 'We always send men to do the job.'

That was all Su Yinling needed to hear. She took a deep breath and explained her plight, hoping that she wouldn't receive an even more gruelling assignment because of her complaint. But the Lord touched Mrs Wang's heart, and she agreed to talk to her husband. Two days later Su Yinling received word that her assignment was being terminated before it had even begun. The farm leader decided to send someone else to feed the pigs. Su Yinling and Han Liding rejoiced as they realised God had given Su Yinling wisdom and boldness to approach Mrs Wang, and had then moved on her husband's heart to cancel the assignment.

'My mother always said, "If you give God what you have, He'll provide everything you need,"' Su Yinling told Han Liding. 'And she always reinforced her words with actions.'

Su Yinling explained, for example, that her parents always taught her the importance of tithing and giving offerings in church. They wanted her to see for herself that God would provide everything the family needed – and she need not fear to obey God in this matter even in times of lack. She remembered sitting beside her father helping him calculate the ten percent of the family income to give back to God – and then helping her mother choose the cleanest coins to give.

'My father would always say to pay your tithes first and then your bills,' Su Yinling said, 'not the other way around. Even after he died, the Lord took care of us. Our friends from church would drop off clothing and money, and we were never in need. Whenever someone gave my mother money, it would go right into the offering basket – always in a red paper wallet, just like the kind we received as children on birthdays and New Year's. She'd always tell us that the Lord's money is inexhaustible.'

The principles that Su Yinling's parents taught her about God's provision proved to be true not only when she was a child, but even years later when she was on a work farm in the middle of nowhere.

Chapter 13

Huiliang's Story

'Some trust in chariots, and some in horses; but we will
remember the name of the Lord our God.'

(Psalm 20:7)

Over and over again Enshi heard similar stories that
encouraged him, but he couldn't help wondering what was
happening to Huiliang. Enshi had no way of knowing that
she was enduring her own round of persecution, beginning
with seemingly endless interrogation not long after Enshi
was arrested. Her sister and brother were also questioned
about their relationship to Enshi, although they were not as
steadfast in their commitment to him as Huiliang was.

'It's your fault that we have so much trouble!' they yelled
at Huiliang whenever the government investigators would
come to their door. 'Why did you have to make friends with
someone like Enshi?'

Huiliang tried to reason with them, but it was to no avail.
There was no escaping persecution at work either. Even
there, investigators would find her and interrogate her for
hours. Over and over, they urged her to turn against Enshi,
but Huiliang always refused.

'You are so stubborn!' they told her, always promising
that they would be back. They added a negative mark to
her file, and ordered her superiors to watch her and let
them know if she did anything suspicious.

In the midst of intense persecution, Huiliang was also

faced with the dilemma of carrying on her Christian witness or pulling back under pressure. But always the Lord gave her grace to be a bold witness for Him – no matter how trying the circumstances. At work, for example, Huiliang faced the difficult decision of whether or not to say grace before eating her lunch of rice and vegetables. Her co-workers already ridiculed her mercilessly for her Christian stance, and doing something as blatant as praying before eating would only give them more opportunities to harass her. Yet she knew Scripture promised if she would acknowledge her Lord before men, He would acknowledge her before her Father in Heaven.

Huiliang decided there was no other choice. She bowed her head and silently prayed before she ate. Sure enough, those around her pounced at the chance to mock her for praying to a God whom they claimed didn't exist.

'This is the People's Republic of China!' they laughed. 'We don't believe in those fairy tales!'

Yet God rewarded Huiliang's commitment to Him. One day a young woman called her aside after lunch just as she was putting away her glass jar of tea.

'Can I talk to you?' she whispered. 'I saw you pray today. I'm a Christian, too, and I want you to know your praying encouraged me to go on.'

It was moments like that that sustained Huiliang and enabled her to live from week to week. One day her work unit supervisor came storming over to her work area and announced that he wanted her to come to his office immediately. Huiliang knew from the tone of his voice that she was in trouble once again – although this time she judged it was worse than usual because he was screaming louder than he had ever yelled before.

'We've tried to reason with you,' he thundered as he pounded a clenched fist on the table, 'but you won't listen. You refuse to give up these foolish beliefs, and you refuse to tell us the truth about Ye Enshi. You leave us no other choice but to terminate your work here and send you to a farm for re-education.'

Huiliang was shocked. In spite of an impeccable work record, she was being officially denounced as an enemy of the state simply because she and Enshi were Christians. But there was, of course, no reasoning with the official. She had to accept his verdict – or else argue and face even worse recrimination. God's hand, she sighed to herself, must be in this somewhere.

It wasn't long before she saw at least part of His plan for her. When she arrived at the farm, she was overjoyed to discover that there were other Christian women who had been sent there also. After having been denied the joy of Christian fellowship for so long, she couldn't believe that she would find it at a labour farm of all places. The enthusiasm of the sisters encouraged her to be bolder than ever about sharing her Christian faith. God gave her a deep desire to reach the other women working on the farm, as well as those in the surrounding village, and some of the women came to know Him because of her witness.

God even protected her in ways that no one but Huiliang could have appreciated. Born and bred in the city, she was petrified of the snakes that other women told her lurked in the tall grass surrounding the farmlands. Long after midnight when the daily indoctrination meetings concluded, the women had to walk back to their barracks through the grass, never knowing when they might cross the path of a snake. In this particular village, snakes were all too common and everyone had been bitten by a snake at one time or another during their stay at the farm.

Night after night, Huiliang would walk home through the tall grass carrying a long bamboo pole that she would swish through the grass ahead of her to scare away any slithery creatures that might be lying in wait. God honoured the 'desires of her heart', because for two years – the entire time she worked at the farm – not only was she never bitten by a snake, but she never even saw one.

Huiliang knew God was protecting her, yet still the years dragged on, and she never knew when Enshi would be released. It would so much have helped to know the length of his sentence, but the authorities would never tell her. Over and over again, God assured her that although she didn't know about tomorrow, He did – and she could trust Him for it. She relied on His strength and grace to help her endure the moments of intense loneliness and uncertainty.

Yet at times the wait became unbearable, and she prayed that the Lord would take her home. Dying, she thought, had to be better than living. But that was one prayer that the Lord refused to answer. Instead, He quietly reminded her of His words to the prophet Elijah as he hid in a cave,

> *'Go, return on your way.'*   (1 Kings 19:15)

And she would ask God for grace to do that. During the years of waiting, two songs were a constant source of encouragement to her. The first was *God's Way*, Enshi's favourite hymn, which constantly reminded her to walk on God's path and to keep faithful to it, no matter how rocky the road or how dark the night. The other was *Jesus Only Is Our Message*. Whenever she was interrogated and the guards shouted the same questions that she had answered countless times before, this was the song that came to her mind,

> Jesus only is our Message, Jesus all our theme shall be;
> We will lift up Jesus ever, Jesus only will we see.
>
> Jesus only, Jesus ever, Jesus all in all we sing,
> Saviour, Sanctifier, and Healer, Glorious Lord and coming King.
>
> Jesus only is our Saviour, all our guilt He bore away,
> All our righteousness He gives us, all our strength from day to day.
>
> Jesus only, Jesus ever, Jesus all in all we sing,
> Saviour, Sanctifier, and Healer, Glorious Lord and coming King.

Jesus is our Sanctifier, cleansing us from self and sin,
And with all His Spirit's fullness, filling all our hearts
within.

Jesus only, Jesus ever, Jesus all in all we sing,
Saviour, Sanctifier, and Healer, Glorious Lord and
coming King.

Jesus only is our Healer, all our sicknesses He bare,
And His risen life and fullness, all His members still
may share.

Jesus only, Jesus ever, Jesus all in all we sing,
Saviour, Sanctifier, and Healer, Glorious Lord and
coming King.*

During the years of waiting, Huiliang was constantly
pressed to forget about Enshi and marry someone whom
the state considered a more suitable husband – someone
who supported the revolution and did not dare turn against
the government as Enshi had. Huiliang's friends and family
were invariably amazed when she refused all such offers.

'Why do you wait for him?' her friends would ask. 'How
can you do it?'

'Because the Lord is the one who sustains me,' she told
them. 'I believe what the Bible says, that *"marriage should
be honoured by all"'* (Hebrews 13:4).

'But there are plenty of other men who have a lot more
to offer than Enshi,' her friends told her. 'Why don't you
marry them?'

Huiliang knew there was some truth in what they were
saying. There were better candidates – if she looked on the
outside – candidates who had more money, better education, and a lot more worldy influence to offer. Some of
them had even proposed to her. Yet she knew the Lord

---

* *Jesus Only Is Our Message* by Albert B. Simpson and J.H. Burke.

hadn't given her any confirmation to give up waiting for Enshi and marry any of the others.

'He's a brother who's suffering for the Lord,' she tried to explain to her friends. 'I don't make the decision to wait for him based on my own strength. It's the Lord's strength. A Christian can't just give up because of persecution. I must continue to walk ahead.'

And she did.

Chapter 14

A Table Before Their Enemies

*'You prepare a table before me in the presence of my
enemies.'*
(Psalm 23:5)

God always has the last word. No matter what injustices
are committed, no matter how widespread or impenetrable
the enemy's domain might seem, the final word is the
Lord's. Through all the long years of their separation,
Enshi and Huiliang held on to this hope. Psalm 23 had
always been their favourite passage of Scripture, and in
spite of everything that happened – in spite of the merciless
persecution and unfounded injustices – they still believed
that God would prepare a table for them in the presence of
their enemies.

In the late 1970s – after Enshi had spent two decades in
prison – the Chinese government adopted a new policy that
allowed religious prisoners to be released under certain
conditions. It did not represent a changed attitude toward
the Church; the Marxists remained hostile to Christianity.
Rather, China's new, more open economic policies meant
that prisoners with skills – whether Christian or not – were
more valuable in the workplace than behind prison bars.*

Freedom wasn't automatic, however. Each prisoner had
to go through an application and screening process. And

---

* For the background to these new policies, please see Chapter 16.

the prisoner himself could not request release; it had to come from a friend or family member. And so Huiliang, who had finally been released from prison herself, submitted the application form while Enshi waited. They both knew that a positive response to the application depended on the prison warden, Wu Shenning, as well as the head of the prison guards. Either one of them could turn down Enshi's case, and he would be stuck in prison for another two decades.

Enshi was particularly concerned about Wu Shenning, who was one of the harshest officials Enshi had come across during his years in prison. One of the reasons for Wu's ill temper, Enshi knew, was his wife, who was completely insane. At times Wu Shenning himself almost seemed insane in his unrelenting desire to see Christians punished with the cruellest forms of discipline imaginable. One day Enshi was finishing up his watered-down dinner when Gu Dongyi, another believer, walked by him and as casually as possible tried to get his attention.

'Enshi!' he whispered as softly as he could so others wouldn't hear. 'Have you heard about Wu Shenning's wife?'

'What about her?' Enshi asked, looking around himself to make sure no one had seen them. Prisoners who spent too much time talking to each other were subject to disciplinary action, and Enshi didn't need any negative marks on his record when he was applying for release.

Gu Dongyi also looked around, then whispered news that came as a complete shock to Enshi, 'Wu Shenning's wife is healed!'

'What!' Enshi caught himself just as he was about to shout out loud. 'What do you mean healed? The woman is crazy – everyone knows that!'

'Not any more,' said Gu Dongyi. 'You won't believe what happened. Some of the house church believers in town found out about her and took her to church. They prayed for her and she was completely healed! And not only that, but she's now a believer, too!'

Enshi was absolutely astonished by the news ... but not as much as when he saw what happened to her husband as a result of the healing. A lifelong atheist, Wu Shenning was at first suspicious of his wife's healing and conversion, but he could not argue with the results: A woman who was once completely crazy – someone whom countless doctors could not heal – was suddenly quite sane.

Slowly Wu Shenning's suspicion turned to curiosity. Although he dared not jeopardise his position by attending church himself, no matter how secretly, he began to watch the believers in prison. His attitude toward them began to change. His persecution of the Christians began to lessen – albeit only by infinitesimal amounts at first, but at least it was a change in the right direction. Day by day, it seemed, his attitude softened even more, so that when Huiliang applied for permission for Enshi to leave, Wu Shenning actually signed the pass.

When the long-awaited day of Enshi's prison release finally arrived, Huiliang took her vacation time from work in order to make the long journey to the prison to take Enshi home. She had filled out what seemed like dozens of papers, and checked and rechecked them a hundred times to make sure there wasn't some tiny error that could halt the release process.

Huiliang walked through the prison gates and up to the entrance where two guards sat behind a dusty window – a thin, nasty-looking man with a permanent sneer on his face, and a woman whom Huiliang recognised as Yang Ruihong. She had heard stories about Yang, how she was one of the cruellest guards in the prison camp, how she hated Christians, how she even shaved one side of prisoners' heads, just to humiliate them.

Yang seemed to be intently reading a magazine, so Huiliang took a deep breath and handed the release papers to the man, who casually tossed them on to his cluttered desk. Huiliang watched as he warmed his tea, ruffled through yellowed documents, and absentmindedly fingered the wooden beads of his abacus – everything it seemed, but look at the papers she had handed him.

Yet Huiliang didn't dare disturb him; Enshi's fate rested in his hands and she had come too far and waited too long to leave without him.

Yet that's exactly what he told her to do. 'Go on home,' he finally said with a wave of his hand. 'He'll follow.'

'But ...' Huiliang started to protest.

'Look, do you want him released or not?' he shouted without even looking up.

Huiliang looked at Yang to see if she would counter the man's dismissal, but she just waved her hand as if to say the matter was closed, and quickly went back to reading her magazine.

Huiliang knew she dared not disobey the guard's command – especially not with Enshi's release being so imminent. Reluctantly she walked out of the prison gate without the man she had come to get. With every mile on the long journey home, she prayed that God would protect Enshi and watch over his release – and that he would be home later that evening.

Hour after hour, Huiliang waited at home, until the sun was long set. The hours dragged on and when dawn finally came she admitted to herself the harsh truth that she had been tricked. Tears fell from her eyes – just as they had so many times during the past twenty years – and she seemed to lose all hope. She sobbed to herself that the guards had no intention of releasing Enshi. The charade of signing papers and filling out countless forms was nothing more than another of their callous jokes.

And now her vacation time was completely gone, and all she could do was pray that Enshi would be released by the time she got home from work later that evening. But there was no Enshi waiting for her that night ... nor the next night ... nor the next. The weeks dragged on, and every month Huiliang wrote to the highest leader of the labour camp, petitioning him to release Enshi. Twelve months passed, then eighteen, and Huiliang took comfort from Scriptures such as Proverbs 21:1 that promised her,

'The king's heart is in the hand of the Lord, like the rivers of water; He turns it wherever He wishes.'

That verse became her prayer as she begged God to turn the heart of whatever 'king' was standing in the way of Enshi's release – be it a guard, a factory leader within the camp, or the head of the camp himself. Interminable days turned to weeks, then months, then years. Finally, after two long years, Huiliang received word that the leader of the camp – the highest official in the facility – had personally signed the papers ordering the guards to release Enshi.

Huiliang knew God had answered her prayers and had indeed turned the heart of the camp leader. Yet as delighted as she was with the news, she knew that signed paperwork was not enough. She could still be turned away at the gate just as she had been two years earlier – with nothing more substantial than the whim of a guard who happened to be having a bad day.

Once again Huiliang prayed that God would make Proverbs 21:1 a reality. As she returned to the prison, she was all too aware that, unless God moved, there was every chance she could return home again that evening without Enshi. As she walked through the prison gates, she still had no plan or leading from the Lord, yet she knew He had heard her prayers. All she could do was wait to see how He would answer.

But Huiliang's tiny spark of hope was suddenly snuffed out when she saw who was in the office that morning. It was none other than Yang, the same female guard who had refused to help her two years earlier.

'This is who You've sent to help me!' Huiliang cried to the Lord. Fighting back despair she had no other choice but to tell Yang why she was there.

'I've come for Ye Enshi,' she stated as calmly as she could, considering the speed with which her heart was racing.

'Haven't you been here before?' Yang asked suspiciously.

'Yes,' Huiliang replied, 'and they told me to go home and Enshi would follow...'

'But he never did, right? Look, if you want him to be released, don't leave without him.'

'But how can I...'

'Never mind what they tell you,' Yang interrupted, looking around to make sure no one heard her. 'If you go home, they'll only change their minds. Insist you'll wait for him, and then refuse to leave until he comes out.'

Huiliang was astonished that someone who was known for being so heartless to believers would actually tell her the secret for getting Enshi released. God had turned the heart of another 'king'. The tears of frustration that had filled her eyes before were suddenly changed to tears of joy as she realised that God had sent help from the very person she dreaded.

Huiliang did exactly as Yang advised her. No matter what the guards told her, she refused to leave until Enshi was by her side. They promised her everything it seemed – telling her he would follow later that afternoon, or by evening, or in the morning. But Huiliang steadfastly held her ground and would not leave.

Finally, after she had waited for what seemed like hours in a dank, dusty office, the door creaked open one more time. Huiliang sighed to herself and braced for yet another guard with yet another reason why she should leave.

But instead of a guard on the other side of the door, it was Enshi. As many times as Huiliang had prayed for this day, the sight of her beloved actually standing before her was almost unbelievable – as if she were watching someone else's dream take place. Yet she knew it was real, that God was smiling down on the two of them, saying, 'It is finished.' After twenty long years, the wait was over. With the guards listening to their every word, Huiliang knew she had to contain her emotions just a few moments longer and wait until the prison was far enough behind them before she could allow herself to rejoice in the moment. For part of the ride back to their village, Enshi and Huiliang spoke in hushed, hurried tones in an attempt to make up for two decades of separation ... and part of it was spent in silence, each simply enjoying the presence of the other. There was no question about the next step that God had for them. Not long after Enshi was released from prison, he and Huiliang were finally married.

Yet God still had one more surprise in store for them. During Enshi's final years in prison, he had worked in the mechanic shop for a man named Zhang Weiming, a loyal communist party member. Although officially Zhang was not to show partiality to any of the prisoners (least of all Christians), he recognised that the believers were good workers – the best he had, in fact.

He didn't know anything about their Bible, but he knew they believed in serving those who were in authority over them. It didn't matter to him why they were good workers; he was just glad they were in his shop because the work they did made him look good to his superiors. These believers were also trustworthy and honest, and he knew if he left them in charge of something in the shop, it would be done when he returned.

And so when Enshi was finally released from prison, Zhang Weiming knew he was losing a valuable worker. What could he do, he wondered, to say good-bye to this man? Finally an idea came to him. He would host a dinner in his home for Enshi and his new wife – not just any dinner, but a banquet complete with the best food available.

God really did prepare a table before Enshi and Huiliang in the presence of their enemies.

Chapter 15

A New Life

'I would have lost heart, unless I had believed that I would see the goodness of the Lord in the land of the living. Wait on the Lord; be of good courage, and He shall strengthen your heart; wait, I say, on the Lord!'
(Psalm 27:13–14)

Perhaps the authorities thought that twenty years in prison would 're-educate' Enshi. Perhaps they thought that after all the years of *pidou* and torture he would never want to join another church again. And perhaps they thought that Huiliang would try to convince her husband to live out the rest of his life in relative quiet by not doing anything to anger anyone.

But two decades of persecution, torture, and separation only strengthened the resolve of Enshi and Huiliang. As soon as Enshi was released from prison, the couple quickly continued the very same activities that got them into trouble twenty years earlier. First they joined a house church. Then Enshi began preaching in underground settings. Next he and Huiliang began distributing Bibles and Christian literature. They even became the drop-off point for westerners who secretly brought Bibles into China.

The local police knew Enshi and Huiliang had contact with many foreigners living in their city as well as relatives and friends overseas, and they watched them intently. The more they watched, the more suspicious they became.

Enshi knew it was only a matter of time before he would be arrested again. Reluctantly he and Huiliang applied for passports to leave China and for visas to enter a western country where some of his relatives were already living. Night after night, they would pray quietly and discuss their plans. Neither one wanted to leave China, preferring to stay and work with the unregistered church. But they knew it would not help their fellow believers if Enshi were arrested again.

The months turned into years while Enshi and Huiliang waited to hear if their passport and visa applications were granted. Finally two years after they had applied, they received their passports, but they could not leave China unless they had visas from the other country granting them permission to settle there. And they still weren't convinced God wanted them to do that.

In the late 1980s, Enshi participated in an evangelistic meeting of 400 people. Three days later, one of the leaders was arrested for distributing literature and training house church pastors. Among the many questions shouted at him during his interrogation sessions were questions asking for details about Ye Enshi. Although he refused to divulge any information, the authorities were convinced Enshi was somehow responsible for the increase of Christian activity in the area.

Pressure against Christians intensified in the following weeks. Just when the situation seemed almost unbearable, Enshi and Huiliang suddenly received notice from the country to which they had applied to immigrate, that their visa applications were approved. They took it as confirmation from God that the time had come to leave China. A sympathetic government official who was a friend of the family advised them to leave quietly without a big family gathering, because of the danger of re-arrest through betrayal. Enshi and Huiliang sadly complied with the warning, leaving China within a few days.

A month after their departure, Enshi learned that government officials had been planning to arrest him again.

Today Enshi and Huiliang are living in a western country where they speak frequently about the state of the unregistered church in China. Invariably someone always asks Enshi how he endured the time of tremendous pain and loneliness while he was in prison. Enshi says there were three reasons.

First, he points to the strong Christian upbringing he received from two generations of elders living in his household – his grandfather, who was converted as a young man when a foreign evangelist came to his village, and his parents who spent hours with him as a child helping him memorise Scripture and teaching him to serve the brothers and sisters in church.

Second, Enshi survived the years of imprisonment because other Christians were praying for him – not only Christians he knew, but those around the world whom he would probably never meet. Even when every missionary had been kicked out of China, when every church building was closed and virtually every Bible confiscated, it was the prayers of believers all over the world that sustained their brothers and sisters locked behind closed doors in China.

And finally Enshi believes he survived prison because even when hell itself seemed to camp outside his cell, he still honoured Jesus as Lord. He knew God had a purpose in everything and was still in control of seemingly out-of-control situations. As a result, persecution and trials actually became blessings because they caused him to lean solely and completely on the Lord.

Huiliang also learned to lean on the Lord in ways that are beyond explanation. Day after day, week after week, year after year without any news about Enshi, Huiliang had no strength of her own to continue. It was Almighty God who carried her through. During the most merciless of times, her life was like the man who saw a vision of his life laid out as a walk along a sandy beach. Most of the years of his life, there were two sets of footprints – his and the Lord's. But during the most difficult times of his life, there was only one set of footprints in the sand. The man complained to God, wanting to know where He was during the times of suffering. The Lord quietly responded that during the most difficult times, the single set of footprints was His own – because He was carrying His child.

For Huiliang and Enshi, there was more than one occasion when there was a single set of footprints in the sand. God worked for them a hidden miracle, one which He has repeated in this time for many believers in China.

Chapter 16

Hidden History

'History hath triumphed over time, which besides it, nothing but eternity hath triumphed over.'
(Sir Walter Raleigh *The History of the World* 1614)

China: The Hidden Miracle could end here, but if it did, it would accomplish only half its purpose. Huiliang and Enshi's story speaks of the triumphs of God who is victorious in every situation. Hopefully their lives have encouraged you in the situations you face. But there is more to their story than that. With one out of every five people on this planet living in China, the Lord is raising up an army of Christians all over the world to serve this enormous country. The Ye's story is designed to encourage you to enlist in that army. You may be called simply to pray regularly for China or you may be asked to travel to the 'front'. As you read the next few chapters, pray that God will show you your part. Whatever it is, you can be sure it is vital. The persecution that the Ye's endured continues unabated in China today. There are still millions of Chinese Christians who face persecution, arrest, imprisonment, torture and even death because they seek to serve Him.

The first step in this process is to understand the historical background to the Ye's miracle. Because it is a **hidden** miracle, many people outside China are still unaware of her recent past and her present situation. That understanding is crucial.

In 1949, the new Marxist leadership of China stated with some truth that China had at last 'stood up'. After years of domination by outside forces, the Chinese were now masters of their own nation and destiny. The 'long march' that had begun for the Communists in the 1920s, which had been almost stalled at times in the '30s and '40s under the Japanese and the Nationalists, now reached its intended destination. October 1st, 1949 saw the birth of a new nation – the People's Republic of China.

However, the Communist Revolution that promised so much was in reality to usher in decades of suffering and struggle. Mao experimented on a grand scale with China's millions, attempting to mould them to fit Marxist theories. The application of these theories led to progress in some areas, but also to bitter and costly suffering for almost all sectors of Chinese society. This continued for nearly thirty years during which time China was almost completely cut off and hidden from the outside world.

A significant swing in direction began to take place in 1976 after the death of Mao. His successor, Deng Xiaoping, sent shock-waves through the Party by introducing fundamentally new economic policies. Known as the 'Four Modernisations', they were designed to rescue an economy strangled by political dogma and to bring China into leadership in the world's market-place by the year 2000. They therefore set Deng's wing of the Party at loggerheads with the hard-liners (the strict followers of Mao), who favoured the classical Marxist economic policies of central control and of State intervention on every level.

Most outside observers made a basic misjudgement at this point. They assumed that economic change would inevitably result in a new political order. Indeed, so radically different was the new financial direction that even some experts believed China was becoming a new addition to the capitalist world. How wrong that was. Though the two wings of the party differ radically on how the economy should be run, they are both totally committed to the same political world-view. Both feared the political consequences that had to be faced during this new era. Their differences lay in the evaluations they made as to the urgency for economic change. Deng was willing to gamble that opening up to the outside world was an acceptable price to pay for the economic benefits. He was persuaded that a tightened internal control could handle any fall-out from that. The hard-liners, however, wanted to downplay the economic factors, arguing that the rule of the party and its ideology were all that mattered.

To facilitate his views, Deng over the years instituted a series of initiatives that were designed to keep strong political control at the centre. Seen in that context, the Tiananmen Massacre on June 4th, 1989 was not inconsistent. Thousands of students (some say as many as two million) had gathered to declare that economic changes alone were not enough. There must be political, even moral change. The irony of the original Tiananmen movement was this: it was not anti-Marxist; rather it was critical of how the current leadership abused their power.

The astonishing and wanton slaying of so many of China's young intellectuals that followed, led to a deep disillusionment and hostility, almost unparalleled in Chinese history. Yet it served to define even more clearly the line that the current regime takes – economic change must be encouraged; political change must be resisted. The 14th Party Congress at the end of 1992 formally enshrined that doctrine for years to come. Indeed the Chinese have a phrase for it: *nei jin wai sung* ('Inside tight; outside loose'). It means that a loosening will be permitted on the outside, in matters relating to economic growth and development. But political change is not on offer – from either wing of the Party. It is clear that there will be no more toleration of 'democracy' or of any prospect of political change until all the old men in the Party have left the scene.

Post-Tiananmen China has witnessed another round of bold economic initiatives by Deng. These have reversed the slowdown caused by the international horror at the 1989 massacre. As a result, China has one of the fastest growing economies in the world. It is as though the events of 1989 were all a nightmare that has passed with the coming of a new day. The economic kings and princes inside and outside of China have closed ranks once more. Today they continue to plan a path that offers the most financial advantage to them all.

Church and State

The Christian church has inevitably been caught up in this maelstrom of political aggression. The hard-liners and the Dengists both share a fundamental hostility to Christianity. The Dengists, however, are more pragmatic in their approach and recognise the nation's need for the skills of Christians. The church for that reason is permitted to exist. But she will most certainly not be allowed to flourish. Policies are in place that are designed to cut the church off from all forms of sustenance – from Bibles, from training and teaching, from relationships with Christians outside (and often inside) China.

It is in this cauldron that the Ye's have lived out their lives and followed their Master. These political events have formed the backdrop to their story. During this period, men and systems have attempted to reshape their lives – but failed. The pressures have come from both government and church. A key element of the government strategy towards the church has been to form an agency for the Party's control of Christianity – the Protestant Three Self Patriotic Movement (TSPM). It is not a church as such, but it is the officially recognised instrument of leadership of China's Protestant church. The Party also sees the TSPM as 'the voice' of the Protestant church in China. Some leaders of the TSPM have, since its inception in the 1950s, undoubtedly been involved in the persecution of the very Christians for whom they should have been caring. The result is that a significant number of ordinary Chinese believers and some of their leaders oppose elements within the TSPM for their highly political agenda.

In some of the TSPM churches there is good preaching, Bible studies and prayer meetings. There are many genuine Christians who attend TSPM churches, who have no idea of the political or spiritual implications of belonging to such a church. There are also a good number of sound, Bible-believing pastors. The issue lies with the top leadership of the TSPM, which is strongly influenced by loyalty to the Party. In the leadership of a TSPM church at the local level, normally one of the leaders will be primarily politically oriented, responsible for seeing that Party policy is adhered to, and the rules are kept. The 'Christ or Caesar' issue – that of Christ being the Lord of His Church – is a continual issue for many in China, as it was and is for the Ye's. Many have looked for places and forms of worship outside the TSPM's control.

'Unofficial' house churches have thus sprung up all over China. The term 'house church' refers to a group of Christians, which may number from ten to more than one thousand members, who meet in venues that have not been registered with the government or with the TSPM. That may be because they live too far from the 'official' churches. Or it may be for reasons of conscience and conviction. Some may integrate with other groups into quite large movements under some form of common leadership. Others may be individual, having little or no contact with other such groups. Some may have functional relationships with the TSPM; others may regard that as biblical apostasy. It is difficult to paint a common picture in this Holy Spirit led growth. But one thing is clear. The vast majority of Christians in China worship in house churches, and not in the TSPM churches.

A Chronological Summary

In order to fit the Ye's experiences into this framework, it will help to look again at all of this from a chronological viewpoint. China's history since 1949 can be divided into four periods, each one of which has significantly affected the lives of millions of people like the Ye's.

1. 1949–1966

This first period was one of control by the hard-liners. Both within the country and on the international scene China adopted increasingly dogmatic postures. These led to repression within the nation and to isolation from the outside world. Brother Ye was arrested in the 1950s for preaching Jesus – in the first period of increasing hostility to the Gospel by hard-liners.

2. 1966–1976

The Cultural Revolution saw the most intense trials and persecution under Mao, the Gang of Four and the Red Guards. To be a Christian in China at this time meant facing much suffering, imprisonment and even death. Brother Ye suffered deeply through this period, facing the merciless hostility of those who believed that Christianity should be purged from the land.

3. 1976–1989

This was a period of economic reform. Deng Xiaoping brought in the sweeping economic changes outlined above, kick-starting an economy that needed to catch up with the rest of the world. Brother Ye was released in this period, because men like him were seen as useful to the economic growth of the country. Their faith in Jesus was never welcomed, but economic growth brought a temporary tolerance of it. By God's grace it was during this period that the church in China experienced a season of phenomenal growth.

4. 1989–today

China's massive economic growth inevitably opened up the nation to the West. There were sights long hidden from many Chinese – that of life outside Maoism. New hopes and ideas swept the nation, both for good and for bad. The brutal suppression of the Tiananmen incident, as has been explained above, clearly defined the limits of that opening. The church has suffered for that. During this fourth period, with fresh political tightening, new threats of arrests have come, with many brothers and sisters once more facing imprisonment for their faith. Their meeting places are once again being closed down and their Bibles and teaching books destroyed or confiscated. Yet in spite of this brutality, the cost to China's economic growth appears to have been only temporary. Today, some sources claim that China has the most dynamic economy in the world. One official with experience in the World Bank has said that by the year 2020, China could surpass both Japan and the USA as the world's largest economy.

The future of China and its church lies in the Lord's Hands – and in those of His praying people. The experts who try to predict the future from the past and present come up with widely different answers. Some are convinced that post-Tiananmen China finally demonstrates that a country can prosper economically without opening up democratically. They argue that the 'opening up' never came and yet China's economy, after the slowdown enforced by international displeasure at the start of the 1990s, is now booming its way back into global significance. Others point to the events of other Asian lands, arguing that economic growth has always led to the emergence of a well-educated and affluent middle class, who will eventually no longer tolerate political repression. Perhaps the answer lies somewhere in the middle – that in time, by some process of transition, a new generation of Chinese leaders will come forward who will see that the good of their land cannot be defined only in economic terms, but must also embrace political change for the good of the individual.

Until that happens, scores of Chinese men and women will continue to experience a Christian life very similar to that of the Ye's. For that reason their story is not merely a glimpse into a forgotten era of China's history that has thankfully taken its place in the museum of man's atrocities to his fellow man. This book reflects China today, as well as China yesterday. It is as much a challenge for prayer and service as it is a reason for praise. May God speak through it to each reader in His sovereign way.

Chapter 17

The Cry Unheard

'Then ... came another sound like the pain of a million broken hearts wrung out in one full drop, a sob. And a horror of great darkness was upon me, for I knew what it was – the cry of the blood.'

(Amy W. Carmichael, *Things As They Are*)

This account of the Ye's pilgrimage must not just impact our minds, nor must it merely stir our emotions. It must come as a challenge to our wills; a challenge that leads to our specific involvement. What is taking place in China may be hidden from us, because it takes place behind a carefully erected bamboo curtain. It may also be remote, because it is happening thousands of miles from where many of us live and quantum leaps away from our normal Christian life-styles. Yet in spite of all that, we must allow this story to come to us as a call to action.

Over the years Chinese Church Support Ministries has sought to define the areas in which Christians from outside China can helpfully involve themselves in ministry to China. We do not wish to be party to a 'hit and run' kind of approach, which may satisfy our ego but does little to benefit those who really need our help. In setting our parameters, we have been careful to submit ourselves to the advice and counsel of those we have met inside China who bear the responsibility for leadership in China's church. How do they see the need? How do they feel we can most be of service? The following three chapters reflect what we feel to be a God-given mandate as distilled from their requests. There are three simple but demanding ways of serving the Chinese church: by voicing her silent cry, by stimulating urgent prayer, and by providing for her nurture and growth.

Voicing the Silent Cry

This first response is best summed up by an incident described in my book *Heartcry for China*. It was an event that helped me to understand God's heart for China and how each of us with a desire to obey Him may recognise that more clearly:

'From a couple in church leadership in China, there came a special word to me – a heart cry from China. "Please be a reporter for us," they said. "We have no means by which our voice can be heard by others, inside or outside of China. Simply say to our brothers and sisters outside of China, 'Some people tell one story, and their voice is heard. But others are telling a different story, and their voice is not being heard.'"'

I considered the couple before me in that simple room. I knew that Mr and Mrs Chen, Renguang and Enhui, were Christian leaders, undertaking to help lead and feed spiritually many believers in and around the city of Shanghai. I knew that they were of an age to have walked through the early days of Marxism in China in the 1950s, followed by the yet more difficult days of the Cultural Revolution in the late '60s and early '70s. That meant that what they said did not come out of an immature or hot-headed enthusiasm. Their words were born out of many years of suffering for the Lord Jesus Christ and for His gospel. I knew also that they loved the Lord Jesus deeply – that their zeal for Him was as real as ever. It was clear that, whatever they might have walked through in the last few decades, their love for Him burned bright.

"Be a reporter for us," the Chens said. They wanted me simply to show Christians outside of China what are the needs of the many, many believers in China's numerous churches. The Chens and many like them do not have a voice to tell you what their needs are, whoever you may be that read this book. You have not gone or cannot go to them, and the vast majority of them cannot come to you. And so they need "reporters" to try, as best we can, to share faithfully what they are saying. We make mistakes, we misunderstand and misinterpret. But we do at least try to serve them. The Chens asked me to be **one** reporter, not **the** only one.

The Chens and many others are frustrated by their lack of a voice. But more than that, they are frustrated by the failure of many believers outside China to understand the need for "reporters" who will give a wider picture of China's church scene. Do we not understand, they might ask, that Marxist governments work by controlling the information that comes out of their country on any subject? Surely after we have seen the two totally different versions of the events in Tiananmen Square in June 1989 (the Chinese government's and that of the world's reporters), we can understand that truth is a highly negotiable commodity in the context of China's state-run media. Do we not see that this serves to hide much of the truth about believers in China too? Will we not listen to them when they say that they would like to have voices that we can hear, for they do not have any voice under that system?

"Be a reporter for us." The words remained with me for the rest of the evening, and for the rest of my time in China. I do not claim to be more than one observer of the China scene – there are others who know much more than I do. But I do claim that God spoke to me that night in Shanghai, and laid a commission upon me to serve the Christians in China by helping others in other lands and other churches to hear their heart cry.'*

The Chen's cry that their voice be heard is as real today in the 1990s as it was then, more than a decade ago. There are two major reasons why Christians misunderstand the situation faced by our brothers and sisters in China. One is created by the selective way in which world events are reported by our media – secular and sometimes Christian. The other springs from a widespread but uninformed political optimism that China is following the same path as the Eastern European nations.

Fading Images

The first and media-related reason why we fail to hear and to understand the voice of China's church has to do with the kind of coverage that has – and has not – been given to China over the last few years. It began with the sights and sounds of China at the end of the 1980s. Many Christians did switch on to China for a few months in 1989. The student demonstrations in Tiananmen Square, the hunger strikers' defiance of the Party bosses, the way that the visiting Gorbachev was pushed from centre stage, all these things astonished and fascinated us. Then amazement turned to sorrow as we grieved and wept together at the massacre on June 4th, 1989 and the events that followed.

But then, just as quickly, we largely forgot. By late 1989 and early 1990 media attention had switched to Eastern Europe, as our startled eyes beheld the collapse of one of the pillars of our modern world – the Soviet Empire. Shortly after that it was the Middle East that stepped into the spotlight, with the invasion of Kuwait, the Iraqi crisis and the war that followed. It was not wrong for Eastern Europe and the Middle East to gain our attention. But it

---

* *Heartcry for China* by Ross Paterson.

was wrong for many of us totally to forget those crucial events in China. The effect of those events in 1989 could not be tuned out in China, in the same way that they had disappeared from our TV screens when media attention focused elsewhere. For Chinese Christians there are real and serious ongoing implications. They live with those consequences, whether we care or not.

It is hard to overestimate the impact of those Tiananmen events on the Chinese people – both the immediate impact and the long-term impact of the government policies they inspired. For better or for worse, the whole of this present period of China's history is being defined around the events of June 1989. In a restaurant in the United States recently I asked a waiter from Mainland China when he had come to America. He simply replied, 'I came out after Six-Four; my wife came out before Six-Four.' 'Six-Four' is of course the 4th day of the 6th month – June 4th, 1989. What other nation's students would give you a month and a day without a year attached to divide and define history? The impact of those events on the Chinese inside and outside of China is incalculable.

If the media do focus on China today, it is in a very selective way. It sometimes seems the only issue of interest is that of the economy and the current boom in business opportunities in China. And, to be fair, that is the impression the China of the 1990s would make on an incoming reporter. A mainland Chinese friend recently returned to China after a gap of two years. She was amazed at how swiftly the standard of living had improved. She told us,

'Everything is so very different from two years ago. People have a much more comfortable life. Many Chinese are now determined that making more and more money is their main aim in life. They must ensure they have enough for their children, grandchildren and great grandchildren. Posters of the money god are everywhere – on the windows of the shops, on the front door of every house. "Getting rich" is the main topic on many television programmes and money god figures regularly appear on the screen. The state seems to condone this superstitious worship.'

In view of this it should not surprise us that *Newsweek* magazine, in an article published just before the 14th Party Congress in Beijing in October 1992, should interpret the trend as follows,

> 'The session runs a strong chance of becoming China's last ruling-party congress ever to call itself Communist. The label already seems spurious.'

China, in the words of another report, is more interested in teaching its people how to make money than it is in instructing them in Marxism or Maoism. Another report tells of the plan to open a US$94 million casino resort. Chinese Government representatives met with officials from Nevada to discuss the proposal. This too sounds like a turning away from communism towards capitalism. It makes good newspaper copy.

What we have to realise, as we watch the news bulletins and read our newspapers, is that the reporters are only telling us what they can see on the surface. (Perhaps they only see what they want to see!) But the fact is that at the same time as the above media reports were coming out, we received a fax from Hong Kong reporting quite different incidents that are totally untouched in the secular press. The fax stated that,

> 'During the past few weeks, there has been a new wave of persecution against the house churches in Central and Southern Henan Province. Many home churches have been surrounded by large groups of PSB (police) officials, everyone in the meeting arrested and taken to detention centres.'

The same source speaks of interviews with several dozen preachers from another region of China,

'Every person told of arrests, beatings, fines, confiscation of not only books but of every item they owned. They are beaten to get them to deny their faith in Jesus ... The government just wants to eliminate Christianity.'

Comparing *Newsweek* and unpublished reports such as that contained in the fax, one is tempted to enquire whether the writers are even reporting on the same country. But that is how China is today. It takes us once more to China's two faces in the 1990s – the face that welcomes those who will help the economy and the other face that threatens those who cross the economic boundary to care for the spiritual needs of her people. The media prefers the open face. They largely ignore the hidden one, at least as it affects China's sixty million or more Christians. But that is a fact of life for Christians and for many others in post-Tiananmen China.

Christians need to accept that the agenda set by our media leaders often does not touch issues that ought to be of real concern to us – such as the right of citizens to worship according to their belief and conscience. It is time for us to break free from this media-created agenda and return to a biblical one. It is time to hold our attention span beyond the prescribed fifteen minutes. It is time to look as Jesus looks upon the nations of the world.

A Wrong Assessment

The second reason why we fail to hear and to understand the voice of China's church has to do with what I have described as 'uninformed political optimism'. The collapse of the Soviet Empire has led to a massive misunderstanding about China. For many Christians outside of China the reasoning runs something like this: If Russia has opened up, then surely China has as well. And the facts do seem to support that. The surface energy in the Chinese economy suggests a new season in the country. Indeed, these folk argue, China is economically stronger than Russia, so she must be further down the same political track.

But the real truth is that Russia and China have for the last decade or more gone in directions that are diametrically opposed to each other. There is a key here that, once understood, makes the whole contrast fall into place. Russia has seen major political change and yet massive decline on the economic front. China has seen vast progress economically while determining not to allow any political winds of change to blow. Their approaches over the last decade to these two fields of change – the economic and the political – have been totally different.

The changes in Russia, far from drawing the Chinese along with them, had a hardening effect on the Beijing leadership. They felt challenged by the power vacuum in classic Marxism that was left by the Soviet Union. Seeing themselves as the leader of the last bastions of Marxist–Leninist thought, they have dug in to hold that line. The astonishing changes in Eastern Europe that followed so quickly upon Tiananmen thus did have a profound impact on the thinking of the Chinese political leadership. Unfortunately it was in precisely the opposite direction to that optimistically assumed by most people outside of China.

One of the main target groups for their hardening policies has been the Christian church. The Chinese felt that the church in countries such as Romania and Poland had played a major role in the changes that took place. So, not surprisingly, they saw their own large and ever-growing Christian population as a real threat to their regime.

Consequently they proceeded to target the church for renewed persecution. Their attitude to religion in general and to Christianity in particular has been hardening ever since. A video by a Xin Hua (New China News Agency) reporter was said to be circulating in the early 1990s showing footage of his experience in Poland. It warned that China would face the same problems as Poland and the other nations if it did not 'strangle the baby (of Christianity) while it is still in the manger.'

The present leaders are making it clear that they will not tolerate any threat to their particular brand of reform. Deng Xiaoping's faction is reported in the *People's Daily** as saying,

> 'Once the factors of turmoil reappear in the future, we will, if required, not hesitate to use any means to eliminate them as soon as possible. We can use martial law or use measures harsher and stricter than martial law.'

It is a clear signal that Deng will not loosen political control.

> 'The turmoil (of 1989) made us further understand the importance of stability for rapid economic growth.'*

Beijing will not relax its iron control over the populace.

A Time to Remember

All of this brings us back with new poignancy today to the commission received from the Chens in Shanghai,

> 'We have no means by which our voice can be heard by others, inside or outside of China. Simply say to our brothers and sisters outside of China, "Some people tell one story, and their voice is heard. But others are telling a different story, and their voice is not being heard."'

Whatever the cause of our deafness may be, we need to unstop our ears and hear what is really going on. The strategic importance of this matter is best illustrated by

---

* *People's Daily* of 27 April, 1992.

taking one example from the many that occur in today's China.

In late 1992, some forty Public Security Bureau (PSB) officers broke up a house church meeting in the southern village of Guofa, Wuyan District, at around 11.30 am, blocking entrances and arresting virtually the entire congregation. Those arrested included local Chinese Christians and three foreign visitors. The three foreigners – an American-Chinese man, a Singaporean woman and a Malaysian woman – were also taken into police custody. The foreigners were accused of 'participating in illegal religious activities' and were put under police investigation. Both the local Christians and the foreigners were 'roughly handled' during the incident.

Some twelve local church members were soon released after they paid for their food and board in prison (RMB66 or about two weeks' wages per person). However, when they returned to their homes, many of them discovered that everything of value had been confiscated. The family that had hosted the meeting found their house was stripped bare. Furniture, clothes, blankets, eating and cooking ware were all taken. Things of little value such as handmade prayer mats and stools had been taken out and burned. All Bibles and Christian literature had been confiscated and destroyed. According to the report, scores of families who were involved in the meeting lost all of their possessions, farm animals and equipment, and were beaten by the PSB officers in the process.

One of the families claimed that if the PSB left anything, neighbours came and stole it, as the Christians were now considered 'counter-revolutionary criminals' who had no legal rights. One woman who suffered severe looting said, 'Even during the worst behaviour of the Japanese armies during the occupation they did not strip our homes bare.'

The American-Chinese Christian was repeatedly interrogated and also restricted to his Wuyang hotel for eighteen days before the authorities eventually released him. Almost all of the Chinese Christians who were detained were repeatedly questioned about their religious activities and were beaten while in custody.

On September 8th, when the raid occurred, the weather was still quite warm and the church members were wearing light clothing. However, when later the nights became very cold, in many instances the PSB officials did not permit family members and friends to bring warmer clothing and food to those in detention. The officials told them, 'You say your God can take care of you and you don't need us communists – therefore you can pray to your God for food and clothes.' In a few cases, families were successful in delivering food and clothing to those in detention, but in almost all cases the authorities demanded RMB200 (or approximately two months wages) per person for this favour.

The significance of this report is that, because there were foreigners present, the voice of this particular group of persecuted believers was heard outside of China and their plight was reported. As a result, strong prayer was made for them. Members of Parliament and others with influence were contacted. Therefore, within a comparatively short space of time all the arrested Christians were released. None were given long prison sentences or charged with counter-revolutionary (or political) crimes. Because of the presence of three caring foreigners, their otherwise silent cry was heard and a response was made. The fact is that the PSB officials were unaware that there were foreigners present when they made the raid. They thought that Christians outside China would never hear about their hidden activities. This time they were wrong. But on other occasions the facts are different. We do not hear.

God answered prayer – prayer that came because the voice of China's church was heard. Listening to their voice is vital – it is the lives and liberty of our brothers and sisters in China that are at stake here.

Chapter 18

Prayer: The Christian's Breath

'The prayer of a righteous man is powerful and effective.'
(James 5:16)

The second step in our response to the Ye's testimony must be prayer. The first step, that of hearing the voice of the church in China, is essential. But it is not enough. It must lead to committed and united prayer for China.

A Fearful Flight of Fancy

I would like to ask you to join me in a dark flight of fancy. Suppose that you are a political leader with a specific agenda. A major part of that agenda is to remove the church of Jesus Christ from your nation. Suppose that you had more or less unlimited powers, powers that were not encumbered by your own national legal code nor by international interference. Nothing stands in the way of your attacks on the Christian church in your land. What steps would you take to achieve your ends?

Your first step might be to silence by intimidation or arrest all national Christian leaders. You might even kill some. Pressure the remainder into joining your version of the church, one that mouths your ideological slogans and not the Bible, one that is committed to putting Caesar (you) before Christ. If they refuse to bow the knee, declare them to be counter-revolutionary criminals. Then using such tools as 'accusation meetings' and 're-education', mobilise your nation's non-Christian population against them.

Then, remove from your country all foreign nationals who do not mouth the ideology of your regime. As for those foreigners who dare to call themselves 'missionaries', execute a few, imprison and rough-up some others. Then expel them all. Intimidate your people to such an extent that they regard ongoing contact with foreigners of any kind, especially the Christian kind, as too dangerous, however much they want and need that contact.

Take over control of all channels of communication – radio, television, newspapers, magazines and so on. Use these media to exalt the glories of your leadership and policies. Frequently broadcast whatever facts there are that make you look good. If there are facts that make you look bad, rewrite them. Truth is to be defined only as that which serves to exalt your regime.

Add to this scenario media control over information about other countries. Continually proclaim that they are in a terrible social and political state – in strong contrast to the reports about the 'blessings' of life under your regime. Naturally, you would use the media to convince your people of two lies regarding the church overseas. Firstly, that hardly anybody believes in Jesus in foreign lands anymore. Secondly, that those who do believe are corrupt, immoral and generally perverse. Programmes that promote your view of the universe should be daily fare for your people. You could even print 'funny' Bibles, which seem to be the real thing, but in fact remove key doctrines and strip others of Biblical meaning.

Close down all churches, meeting places, Gospel halls and any other form of gathering place for Christians. Set in motion a neighbourhood-watch scheme that encourages your citizens with rewards to turn in any Christians who might meet together in any way whatsoever. Let them report any sounds of worship and of hymn singing. If they see their neighbours reading the Scriptures or engaged in

Daniel-like prayer, then let them hand them in for Daniel-like punishment.

Of course you would totally eliminate the preaching of the Gospel from your land. Ban all evangelism – whether it takes place in a public context of any kind (churches or other venues) or in private conversations (in the streets or homes or elsewhere). Encourage your citizens to report to your security forces any attempt at group or personal evangelism. Reinforce that by giving horrific and very public punishment to any person handed over to you for such a crime, so that those who report them know that their faithfulness to you will be rewarded by harsh criminal proceedings against the Christians and by personal promotion and rewards for themselves. Especially encourage that kind of betrayal amongst relatives and close friends. In so doing, engender such an insecurity amongst Christians that they will never be sure whom they can trust. Bring them to the place where witnessing for Jesus carries such an enormous personal risk that even the boldest waver.

Take this a step further. Infiltrate the churches with those who can mimic prayer and Bible study, who can speak in such a way that even Christians think they are genuine. Have them lie low for long periods of time, working their way into church leadership, whilst being totally faithful to your government and not to the church of Jesus Christ. All the time let them be reporting to you and providing lists of believers who are on fire for Jesus.

When the time is right, have these men and women take over the churches, openly preaching your political gospel and implementing your 'doctrines'. For example, make sure that they deny God's creation of the world; that they are silent about or deny the biblical version of the end of the world and the return of Jesus Christ. Of course they must scoff at miracles, especially the resurrection of Jesus Christ from the dead. Have them state often and clearly that working with you is the real underlying meaning of Christianity. Create through all of this an environment where the fear of man (you) is far greater than the fear of God.

At the same time, target genuinely godly church leaders for special treatment. Publicly attack the best of them as enemies of the people. Do this on a national scale so that the very men and women who should be most respected in your society are seen as the dregs, as non-persons in your new order. Attack them insidiously on a local level too, by spreading totally false stories about them – that they have huge foreign bank accounts that they fund with money stolen from the church; or that they have immoral life-styles. Discredit them with the full force of your underground rumour network. Once again, truth is totally unimportant. You have the mechanism to write your own version of truth.

Meanwhile, go for your nation's youth. Compel them to become members of the youth movement of the Party. Make it clear that they will never get further education or good jobs if they are not active in your cause – especially if they attend church or believe in Jesus. Ban them from church, and also ban any teaching of key biblical doctrines to them. Encourage them to believe that God and science are totally contradictory, that man (especially you and your party) are masters of the universe. Since they are already ignorant of the world outside, they will easily accept that other nations have given up believing in God too, especially those nations that are scientifically advanced. Bring them to the place where they would think it inconceivable that a national leader or a famous scientist would ever read the Bible, believe in God or worship Jesus Christ.

Finally, round up and destroy all Bibles, hymn books and Christian literature, whilst closing your borders to the import of fresh supplies. Ban your printers on pain of fearful punishment from printing any such materials. Ban your citizens from listening to any overseas radio stations impertinent enough to broadcast the Gospel...

So much for our gruesome flight of fancy. Using such methods and more, any political leadership with such an agenda could be very certain to remove the church of Jesus Christ from their land – or so it would seem.

More Members than the Communist Party

In fact, that is precisely what the government of China has done over the last half century. I do not believe that there is any action listed above that it has not taken against the church of Jesus Christ in one way or another, or at some time in the history of their regime. As I wrote the scenario above, I was thinking of specific names and places in which such tactics have been used. Faced with that kind of onslaught, we might deduce that the church of Jesus Christ had been wiped out of the land, or at least reduced to a cringing and hidden minority group. Indeed at the height of the Cultural Revolution in about 1974 the *South China Morning Post*, one of Hong Kong's most respected newspapers, ran an article along those lines. With little news coming out of China in those days, they assumed that the church was dead.

They were wrong. We all were. The church, far from being obliterated, was poised for a period of astonishing growth. The fact is today that China's church is probably the fastest-growing in the world. As the smoke of the Cultural Revolution cleared, there emerged an astonishing view of the Chinese church. The government itself has admitted that by the early 1990s there were over sixty million Christians in China. That means that there are more Christians than there are members of the Communist Party in China – and, incidentally, than there are Christians in the USA or in all the lands of Europe combined. A few years ago the then vice-president of China, Wang Zhen, said that the places of worship in a village in Hebei's Chengan county were bustling with life during the twice-daily Christian meetings, while meetings organised by the party cells were poorly attended, despite the fact that proceedings were relayed by broadcast system and each attendee was paid one yuan. The church in China is very much alive.

How can this possibly be so? How could the church suffer all the attacks I have outlined above, and yet, instead of dying, be full to bursting with resurrection life? It defies logic – human, but not biblical logic. There is one most obvious reason for what we have witnessed. That is **prayer**. I am convinced that the Chinese church has grown so much, and is still continuing to see revival in some parts, because of the commitment to prayer in the corporate and individual lives of Chinese and other Christians. Let me tell you why I believe that.

After 1949, leaders were removed, imprisoned or killed. Missionaries from abroad were forcibly ejected from the land. Chinese Christian leaders inside China, as well as foreigners now separated from their beloved China, could do nothing for her as they watched – except pray. Multitudes of Christians in the churches of China were left with little they could or dared do – except pray. And pray they did. With all that united and desperate prayer, no wonder China is seeing revival today!

Dr E. Stanley Jones, the famous missionary to India, once said,

'If I had one gift, and only one gift, to make to the Christian Church, I would offer the gift of prayer, because everything follows from prayer.'

It would seem that God, who gave prayer as one of His great gifts to this beleaguered church, has by that enabled her to fare much better than the churches of many other nations.

China, this huge canvas in the world today, is one on which God has chosen to paint a clear message: where dependence on Him is expressed in desperate, trusting, united and unusual prayer, He will express Himself in unusual power that cannot be explained and cannot be matched in any other way.

Recently I was in a church with a stained glass window on which was written three simple words: 'Watch God work'. China is a great place to do that. Why pray for China? Because we can see the astonishing results of the actions of God already in answer to prayer for China. Prayer works. In answer to it, God works.

What an exciting prospect – co-operating with God in believing prayer, teaming up with Him to change those things that need to be changed, and watching in breathless admiration and amazement as He enters through our prayers to change the world. Things happen when we pray.

All of this sounds wonderful. Then why, in so many lands outside of China, do we not pray like that? Why do we not learn the lesson? Why do we not believe Brother Ye's comment that the prayers of Christians outside China sustained him while he was in prison inside China? I want to suggest three reasons:

Firstly, our situation, on the surface, is so different from that of China

It is so hard for many of us in 'free' societies outside of China to come to a place of real dependence upon God. After all, our churches seem to be doing quite well – we can gather big crowds, we have our successes. Do we really need to pray? Consider this striking analysis by Selwyn Hughes of the church in Britain (equally true, I suspect, of many other nations),

> 'When people ask me how close we are to experiencing a spiritual revival in Britain, I usually say that at the moment I do not think we are close because the Church is too strong. We have achieved great prowess at organising conferences and rallies. We can bring together huge crowds into some of the biggest auditoriums in our land. We rattle our sabres and make a great song and dance about how the Church is growing. But the truth is that we are pathetically weak. We give the impression that we are strong but people see us as being strong in human terms and not strong in God.
>
> There is great talent in the British Church – talent such as I have never witnessed before – but a lot of it (not all) is talent that draws attention to itself rather than to the Lord. If only the strong in talent and

temperament would see that their strength must be soaked in prayer, then we would see a demonstration, not of the strength of man, but of the strength of God.'*

What a contrast with China. Because the Chinese church has known total weakness and helplessness, it is seeing great evidence of the power of God. Churches in other countries, like Britain, think they are strong, but are in fact weak in terms of God's sovereign activity manifested in answer to prayer.

Secondly, when we pray, we have the wrong priorities

In 1 Timothy 2:1–6, the apostle Paul instructs us to pray for kings and all in authority, for governments and those who rule the nations. That is very applicable to China. Paul adds a powerful word into that equation – the Greek word *proton*, translated in both the King James version and the New International Version as 'first of all'. The word is used fifty-seven times in the New Testament. Fifty-one of those uses are translated 'first' in the English. The basic meaning of the word is given as 'firstly in time, place, order or importance.' Such a small phrase; such a dynamic and revolutionary challenge to our prayer lives. It says God wants us to be a people of the nations in our praying, who for the Gospel's sake pray for the nations 'first of all' (in time, place, order and importance), before we pray for our own concerns. The simple question that emerges from that is: 'Am I doing in my prayer life what God told me to do?'

1 Timothy 2:2 tells us why He wants that – so that nations and peoples (including Christians) can live peaceful and quiet lives. That in turn is for a specific reason. Verse four says that God wants all men to be saved. Peaceful conditions in a nation enable Christians to get on with the job that the Master gave them – preaching the Gospel all over

---

* *Every Day With Jesus*, 13 May, 1991.

their nation and beyond. Division of any kind in a nation, especially that caused by bad government, brings tension and civil strife that distract from the Gospel.

With these truths in mind, China can surely claim a little more of our prayer time. It has a population of over a billion people, or almost a quarter of the world's population. Each day 43,904 babies are born in China. One in every three non-Christians is Chinese. Some estimate that 25,000 people are turning to Christ each day in China. But even at this amazing pace the natural birth rate is outstripping Church growth. Among these new Christians there is a tremendous hunger for the Word of God. However, many believers do not have a Bible or any teaching materials – sometimes even those who seek to lead the churches. It is easy for heresy to arise.

At the same time, as must be obvious from the Ye's story, the church is suffering great persecution. Many are imprisoned for their faith. There are clear signs today of a distinct erosion of the limited freedoms that China's church has enjoyed in recent years. For a number of reasons, the situation is not stable. China's history has been marked by a series of violent upheavals. It is a potentially turbulent and often war-torn nation. There is real potential in China for massive unrest, with unthinkable cost in terms of human lives. The Tibetan, Mongolian, Islamic and other minorities within China are political volcanoes. China's leaders need great wisdom if the more than fifty such minority groups within the People's Republic of China are to co-exist in peace, or to resolve their yearnings for independent nationhood.

On one of my visits to Shanghai, a brother I had come to see was out of town for a day or so. I had been asked to take some Christian books in to him. I therefore spent some of the enforced waiting time looking at those books. There, in central China, I read these words by Oswald J. Smith, the renowned former pastor of the People's Church in Toronto. Though he wrote these words around 1965, they still speak with great authority into the world-wide scene today,

'Has the Church of Jesus Christ lost its world-wide vision? Does the spirit of the great apostle no longer dominate it? ... To go to a church and find its vision entirely localised has been one of the saddest experiences of my travels. Such a church can hardly lay claim to being New Testament in any true sense of the words ... Occasionally a church sees its own town or city and works for its evangelism. A few see an entire state or province. Here and there is one with a nation-wide vision. But oh what a joy it is to find one with the world as its parish. And that – a world-wide vision – is what we need today more than anything else.

Paul said "I must also see Rome." And Rome was farther from Jerusalem in Paul's day than the North Pole is from the South Pole today. Then, too, he planned to visit Spain. You couldn't keep Paul in Palestine just because there was still work to be done there. He was an itinerant missionary and a spiritual explorer for God. Moreover, Jesus had His mind on the 'other sheep' and 'other villages'. When He died, He died for a world. When God loved, He loved the world. He "so loved the world that He gave" – a world gift ... When Wesley said "the world is my parish," he was but expressing this world vision which is so essential today.

It is always easy to tell when a church has a world-wide vision. The prayer meeting is one of the acid tests. Listen, if you will, to the petitions. In the average meeting for prayer, they centre around the local church and the individual needs of the people. But when a church has caught a world-wide vision, the prayers of the people will be world-wide in scope. Petitions will be offered for missionary societies, missionaries whose names have become familiar. Others will take the place of self. Thus the prayer meeting determines the vision...

How can a church get a world-wide vision? By inviting someone who has travelled to its pulpit. By

enabling its pastor to visit the mission fields of the
world. By definitely planning for and working out a
world-wide programme of evangelism. By hanging a
large missionary map of the world on the wall. By
making a financial investment in the regions beyond
and watching results. By holding an annual missionary
convention, and taking up faith promise offerings. By
looking at missionary pictures. Thus, a new interest
will be created and a world-wide vision imparted.

God give us the vision – a world for our parish. Help
us, O Lord, to lift up our eyes, and to look on the
fields, already white unto harvest. "Go ye into all the
world," Thou didst say. Make us obedient. When
Thou didst see the multitudes, Thou wast moved with
compassion. Oh God, what about us? Are we, too,
moved? Have we a world-wide vision?"*

How relevant those words seemed to me in that room in
China as I read them. How relevant they still seem. Is it not
time that we did what God said, reorganised our private
and public prayer life around God's global concerns, and
prayed first for the things that matter first to Him?

Thirdly, we argue that prayer for the nations is a specialised ministry

We live in an age of specialisation. The danger is that we
misapply that trend and give ourselves excuses by non-
biblical thinking. For example, we agree with the idea of
praying for the nations, but we say is it some 'special
calling' of a few. We argue that they have special gifting,
and that they should be encouraged to pray while the rest of
us get on with what we consider to be our 'callings'.

Whilst it is true that some are called to prayer in a deeper
way than others, and also that God divides out different
nations amongst His praying people, yet that application of

---

* *Battle for Truth* by Oswald J. Smith.

'specialisation' will lead us to deny the reality of a biblical truth. In Acts 6:4 the leaders of the Early Church put prayer before everything – even their teaching ministry. That was not because they had a special prayer ministry, but because of their walk with Jesus. They had watched Him put prayer before and above everything. That is why they said to Him, *'Lord, teach us to pray'* (Luke 11:1, NIV). Halfway through their time with Him on earth something suddenly clicked – all that Jesus did was born and empowered out of prayer. They had better learn how to pray if they were going to be able to be of use to Him.

It is also clear from the Bible that even when the Early Church gave themselves to prayer, God had to break in to remind them of the need to focus that prayer on the nations. He wanted those Early Church Christians, if they insisted on specialising, to specialise on praying – and acting – for the nations. Peter was given that strong reminder by the Lord while in prayer in Acts 10. When that failed to impact the church as it should have done, the newly emerged Antioch leadership received an equally clear reminder from Him in Acts 13:1–3.

The impression cannot be avoided that God constantly breaks in to remind us to pray and care for the nations. The question must still be answered as to whether we in this generation will be like the church in Acts 11:2–3 or the church in Acts 13:1–3. The implications are very wide. Prayer and action for the nations are not the specialised responsibility of a few experts. They are the responsibility of the total church.

I have not the space for the practicalities about prayer for China in this book. Obviously there are various expressions of such prayer – as individuals, committing ourselves to pray regularly on our own, in a small group with others who share our burden for that land, in our church groups as we tell others of the situation there.

Chinese Church Support Ministries can help if you require further advice. May I suggest that you take two simple steps:

Firstly, obtain a copy of my book, *Heartcry for China*, and read chapter 6 especially, where there is fuller material on how to pray for China. Obtain Patrick Johnstone's *Operation World* and other helpful books.

Secondly, look at the addresses in Appendix B at the end of this book and find the national Chinese Church Support Ministries address that is most convenient for you. Then write to us. CCSM produces a regular monthly prayer letter (in both English and Chinese). We also produce a China Prayer Update tape every quarter. Both of these encourage informed prayer for China. Derek Prince Ministries – China/Mongolia also produces regular prayer material on China. Please see the listing in Appendix B for national addresses to obtain this material. If that is not enough, we can put you in touch with other groups who publish good materials written out of a similar burden for China and its church. CCSM is strongly committed to raising up prayer for China. We want to help you to be a part of that.

Listen to the voice of one shepherd of the flock of Christ in China,

> 'Many foreign friends ask me how they can help the Chinese church. I answer them with one word: "Pray!" Pray for the Lord's witness in China, for the new converts all over the country. Pray too for the Lord to raise up new pastors. Lift up the leaders of China in prayer because the hearts of the kings are in the Lord's hands. And pray for Bibles. May the Gospel's door be opened ever wider for the millions in China that still don't know Christ.'

Another pastor expressed confidence in the results of such prayer,

> 'I am told by many visitors that Christians around the world are praying for China. I am confident that, because of this intercession, our God, the God who answers prayer, will bless us here in China.'

Would it not be a tragedy if this brother in Christ had been wrongly informed? What if his expectation of the Lord's response in answer to prayer were to be dashed on the rocks by our failure to pray for China?

Chapter 19

For Her Nurture and Growth

'We have nothing. No pastors, no churches, no Bibles
– nothing. We have only God, and so go to Him in
desperation.'
(Wang Mingdao)

We have established that our first response, listening to
the cry of the church in China, will alert us to her situation.
Prayer, our second response, enables us to carry her before
the throne of grace. There we will hear the authoritative
voice of the Lord of the Harvest. But we must not stop
there. Those two steps should lead us into specific action to
meet the needs of China's nation and her fast-growing
church. Practical action, then, must be our third response
to the Ye's testimony.

The Bible makes it clear that faith, if it is real, will
produce works. The order is vital. Most of us are aware that
works must never precede faith. Works that are acceptable
to God will have come out of the place of faith. That is why
our second response, which involves spending time in the
presence of the Lord in a posture of faith, is so important in
this matter. Yet we have to carry a fundamental attitude
out of the place, an attitude which compels us to affirm that
it is biblically inconceivable to listen to God and then to do
nothing. A non-responding church is – or biblically should
be – a contradiction in terms.

Paul, in one of the greatest passages in the New Testament on the subject of faith, makes this very clear,

> *'For it is by grace you have been saved, through faith –*
> *and this not from yourselves, it is the gift of God – not*
> *by works, so that no one can boast. For we are God's*
> *workmanship, created in Christ Jesus to do good*
> *works, which God prepared in advance for us to do.'*
> (Ephesians 2:8–10, NIV)

Paul defines both content and order: faith comes before works; works will flow out of genuine faith. So important in the purposes of God are these good works that He prepared them for us even before the universe existed. The imperative upon us therefore is that we should walk in obedience to that which the God of all grace has prepared for us.

Paul's life is such an eloquent testimony to that reality. His life was steeped in prayer. He spent time with God; he walked in faith. He defined that life for himself and others by saying that *'whatever is not of faith is sin'* (Romans 14:23). But he was also a man of action. He was a church planter, an evangelist, a teacher, a pastor, an apostle, a writer, a father in Christ and many other things. What he taught he also lived out in specific, practical and costly action. Faith is there written large in Paul's life; but so also are all manner of actions arising out of that faith.

I am not suggesting that every Christian has to be involved with China's church – although you need to be open to that, allowing God to touch your heart through the pages of this book. The principles related here to China will apply equally to other areas of God's world. If we are not touched by the cries of the nations around us, it is hard to see what dynamic relationship we have with Paul, Peter, John, Philip and a host of others in the New Testament – or indeed with the Lord of the Harvest Himself. When Thomas the Doubter walked tall again, it was, according to tradition, to go to the nation of India. When John Mark had failed and then been restored by the loving hand of Barnabas, it was to return at once to the task of mission. So Paul, who had once in Acts 15 refused to take John Mark on a missionary journey, later laid claim to him for the Gospel and for his ministry to the nations (2 Timothy 4:11).

This chapter lists some of the ways in which we can serve the church in China. Chinese Church Support Ministries (CCSM) and Derek Prince Ministries (DPM) are involved to one degree or another in all of them. They are therefore approved and tried avenues of action. For reasons of space there are only brief introductions to each ministry. For further suggestions write to any of the addresses listed in Appendix B.

1. Christian literature for China

The first category of specific action for China and her people is that of the provision of Bibles and Christian literature.

It is hard to convey the massive need for Bibles and teaching materials that exists in China today. Many of us are used to having our bookshelves overloaded with Bibles in different versions and with more Christian books than we can ever read. But in China that is hardly ever so. It is only the privileged few who enjoy anything like that kind of abundance. Speaking about the great hunger for the word of God in China, one believer said,

> 'The need for Bibles and for good solid teaching material is so acute ... It is a tragedy that in many areas up to one hundred believers have to share one Bible. Preachers have ridden their bicycles sixty miles to attend meetings, asking for Bibles and books to take back to their districts where thousands of believers share a few books. We could only give them between two and five books. "How can we feed our flocks with just these?" they cried.'

The problem begins with the availability of the Bible itself. In some areas there may be fewer Bibles even than the one hundred-to-one ratio in the statement above – sometimes as little as one Bible for about one thousand

Christians. Many of the letters received from believers within China reveal just how urgently Bibles and Christian literature are needed there. A letter to a Christian radio station outside of China says,

> 'Please send us more Bibles and other spiritual booklets. We have a preacher here who does not have any material to help his preaching.'

Another said,

> 'I wish I could learn God's word by heart. But I do not have a good memory. I would love to have a Bible. My greatest wish is to possess a Bible. I have tried different ways to get a Bible but could not obtain one.'

Yet another wrote,

> 'The Christians here are new babes in Christ. Bibles are insufficient. Many were copied by hand. Without spiritual materials the ministry is very difficult. Many Scripture passages need to be understood. I pray that you would increase our spiritual materials to help us study the Bible.'

A significant number of Bibles is being printed inside China by the Amity Press in Nanjing, which is assisted by the United Bible Societies. But it is a fallacy to conclude that the need will be quickly met by that source alone. Leaving aside the thorny issue of believers having to register for those 'official' Bibles, a brief foray into the field of mathematics soon reveals that the numbers do not add up. Over the last decade or so about five and a half million Bibles have been printed inside China, mostly by Amity. If we add to that an optimistic estimate of the number of Bibles brought into China from all outside sources over the same period, we would then add about four million. Averaging that out to an annual rate over the last decade, we finish with an estimate (almost certainly exaggerated) of less than one million Bibles per year being made available to Christians in China.

Yet there are now over 60 million Christians in China (according to claimed leaks of government figures), with a growth rate estimated by some sources to be at least 3.5 million new babes in Christ every year. Less than one million new Bibles a year means that the supply is not even keeping up with current church growth. Far less is it meeting the backlog of 'older' Christians who have never had a Bible. According to these figures, even if every believer were able to get his or her own copy of the Bible (which would demand a minimum increase of 500% on the level of the last decade), that still would not provide for the millions of new Christians who will be coming to Christ while we are catching up with the believers there already are in China today. So an 850% increase in the supply of Bibles would not be unrealistic! And even if that were met, that still would leave the one thousand million Chinese who are as yet unbelievers, and who may never have access to the Word of God. We can safely say that there is a desperate need for Bibles in China today.

But the problem does not stop with Bibles. There is also a need for three distinct kinds of Christian literature. Firstly, materials to assist in leadership training are essential. Christian leaders in China, like leaders in any nation's church, need help that they might be built up and taught, thus becoming qualified to teach others. Secondly, a massive supply of materials for nurture and teaching in the word of God is needed, suitable for all Christians. Thirdly, various forms of evangelistic material are urgently required. These must be 'various', because naturally the types of materials needed for reaching children, semi-literate adults (who comprise 25% of China's population) and the intellectual elite will differ totally in nature and content.

Many heresies have arisen in the Chinese church because of the lack of good teaching materials. One report tells of a man who convinced people that Jesus would appear to them at a nearby river. This confidence trickster, having taken their money, departed with the excuse that he needed to take this good news to other places. Some of the villagers, having waited all day, waded into the water, fearful that they might be in the wrong place. Unable to swim, they were swept away and drowned. Women have attempted to sacrifice their sons in an imitation of the Old Testament account of Abraham and Isaac. Some leaders teach that people must hear the voice of God audibly in order to receive salvation. This has led to suicides by followers who were desperate because they had not heard God's voice.

Distressing though these stories of error and their sad results might be, they are understandable. Zeal for the Lord and ignorance of His word can be a dangerous combination. One Chinese house church leader put it this way,

> 'People are so hungry for spiritual food that they can easily be drawn into groups with false teachings, without having the skills to discern the truth.'

CCSM and DPM are involved in translating and printing Christian literature for China. We play a significant part in this battle. Yet however much we do, we cannot begin to hush the cry from our brothers and sisters inside China, *'We need more!'*

A logical response to this might be to say that the majority of Christians outside China cannot be involved in this literature work, because they do not speak the language or understand China and its people. That is not true. Each and every believer can do something. The task is too monumental to be left to the 'experts'.

There are at least two specific things we can all do – pray and give. Prayer is required because the production of tens of thousands of Bibles and books for China is a major spiritual battle. The devil contests such efforts, because they will harm his work. Groups of Christians outside of China are needed to take up such projects and pray them through. They will be able to rejoice in a special way at the blessing that will bring to thousands of Christians in China.

Secondly, Christians outside China can help to raise finance for Bibles and for literature projects. Groups can make a specific book project their own special challenge, seeking by every means to raise funds for it. They will 'own it' as theirs before God. These individual and church initiatives in fund-raising are vital. There is plenty of scope for many to use their God-given entrepreneurial skills. It is easy to feel overwhelmed by the enormity of the need. But all of us can respond when given a specific mountain to climb, a realistic target to reach. A specific book project can be just one such target. There is a sense of real achievement for a group to see a book go through the different stages – translation, checking, typesetting, printing and so on. There is the final reward of knowing that books will be so important to believers in China. Churches can easily 'adopt' strategic books, suitable for China, perhaps written by their pastor or someone known to them. CCSM can co-operate with them in such projects.

Again, there is always a need for translators and checkers of the materials in this field of literature for China. Only a minority of those reading this book will have the required skills – fluent English and Chinese, gifting in the area of literature and so on. But such people are vital.

The purpose of this chapter is to stimulate action. What would the Lord have you do, as an individual or a group? The voices from China are clear and urgent,

> 'One of the hardest things about my job is that, after I have planted a church, I have the painful task of telling the newly converted villagers that they may have to wait years before they can have a copy of God's word.'

Another believer said,

> 'In the last three years I have longed for good books. But they are nowhere to be found. I am the only evangelist in this area.'

Write to the ministries listed in Appendix B for further information on any of these matters.

2. Courier or 'donkey' work into China

Many of these Bibles and Christian books are carried over the border into China by individual Christians from other countries. These individuals are called 'donkeys' after the animal that carried Jesus through the streets of Jerusalem. The requirements for such 'donkeys' are that they should have a burden for the people of China, a willing and obedient heart – and arms that can pick up heavy suitcases. No knowledge of Chinese is necessary. You can travel to Hong Kong or elsewhere either as an individual or as part of a team. You can stay for any length of time – a few days, several weeks or many months!

Most people are able to make several trips into China during their stay. These may be short cross-border runs lasting only a few hours, longer trips to Canton for a day or two, or even further excursions deeper into China. Couriers are accompanied by a team leader who has experience of travelling in China.

Invariably, couriers are greatly blessed by their trips. There are frequent stories of the Lord's supernatural provision. One sister, who has been into China many times, said,

> 'One thing never changes – the faithfulness of our Lord. He calls, He equips, He enables and provides every need. Each time He teaches me some new lesson.'

Another courier told CCSM,

> 'I wouldn't have missed it. I wouldn't change anything, as I believe the Lord led us every step of the way ... In (our home countries) we never reach our limits, so rarely need to see the Lord take over.'

CCSM organises regular courier trips to China from various countries. Please contact us if you are interested in joining one of these trips.

3. Christian radio work into China

The Communists may have built the Bamboo Curtain, but they have not built a roof. There are 380 million radio sets in China, many of which are able to receive broadcast signals carrying God's word. The fundamental value of these radio messages cannot be overestimated.

As with literature work, there are three main target areas – training leaders, teaching Christians the word of God, and reaching the lost with the good news of Jesus. Apart from its ministry to those who already know Christ, radio is also a strategic way of reaching China's vast population (now over one billion) with the Gospel. There are a large number of Chinese people who know very little about Christianity. They do not have the facts with which to make a decision for God. Many still consider Christianity to be a foreign religion, totally unsuitable for China. Others believe the Communist propaganda that all religion is superstition. Yet at the same time many are disillusioned and are seeking a new meaning to life. Christian radio ministry can help to answer their questions and doubts, and give them the opportunity to turn to Christ – including those Chinese in rural areas who are still functionally illiterate and will never be reached through 'print' evangelism.

Responses to these radio programmes are very encouraging. The Christian radio stations in Hong Kong regularly receive letters sent to them from inside China. One listener wrote,

> 'I was deeply moved by the Holy Spirit after listening to your programme for half a year. I have since become a Christian and started to know and love Jesus.'

Another wrote,

'I have been a faithful listener to your programme for many years. The Gospel programme is used by God to impart His grace to us. In our pagan society, without the radio Gospel programme we would hardly have a chance to know God; even if we believe, without the radio Gospel we could not get spiritual nourishment. Your radio ministry is very important, very precious. I was converted one evening in 1974, after accidentally tuning in to your programme.'

Contact CCSM or DPM–China for further information on this ministry.

4. Christian professionals working inside China

During the past fifteen years there has been a gradual opening up inside China. As a result there are increased opportunities for qualified professionals from overseas to go and work in various positions within the country. Although the door is firmly closed to 'missionaries', the authorities have sometimes accepted professionals even though they knew them to be Christians. Recognising the quality of their life, they have said, 'Send us more like yourselves.' This provides a tremendous opportunity for Christians to let God's light shine in China.

Christian professionals will be expected to serve the people of China with complete integrity. They are required to share and use their skills and expertise. The quality of lifestyle of such workers is very important. Since it is not only Christians who are working as foreign professionals in China, the difference in lifestyles between Christians and non-Christians should be obvious. Qualities such as truth and love stand out in such a society. Christian professionals will need to live in a very simple way without complaining, even though many modern conveniences available to them at home will not be provided.

China is an atheistic country. Activities such as open evangelism or church planting are not permitted – even though they are legal constitutionally. Yet there is a real spiritual hunger in China which makes personal witness easier than in many other countries. It is easy to get into conversations in the classroom, in social settings and whilst travelling. Openness will increase as trust is built up. Christian professionals will have contact with key Chinese officials, and the quality of their life may give them a chance to witness. Teachers may have the opportunity to speak in more depth with individual students. Young people are usually more willing to share privately and in small groups than in front of an open class of fellow students.

Workers are needed in many fields, both short and long term. However, the most common and easy route into China is as a teacher of English. There is a real thirst for the learning of English in China today. It is a pre-requisite for advance in some fields. It is also a window into another world. This need opens up doors of opportunity for many from other lands to go to China, even those for whom English is not the first language. It may take time for such Christians to obtain the necessary credentials, but it can usually be done.

There are various other areas of possibility, such as medicine, computing and other specialisations. They usually require a higher level of professional qualification. They are also more limited in number, but they do offer real possibilities.

CCSM seeks to link interested parties with groups that can help professionals find their way into China.

One of the first Christians to go to China challenged the people of his day with these words,

'Give up your small ambitions and come to China!'

Now many years later, there are still great opportunities to serve Jesus Christ in that land.

5. Outreach to Chinese scholars living and working outside China

There are thousands of students and scholars from the People's Republic of China now studying in many nations outside of China – in Australia, Germany, the UK, the USA, as well as in many other lands. These are the elite of China's students. Many will occupy leadership positions when they return home. Their stay here could be their only opportunity to hear the Gospel. What a tragedy if that opportunity is lost!

Life for these scholars is not easy. They may well be lonely and disorientated and they usually appreciate any help they are given. There are real opportunities to show them God's love in action. This could include inviting them for a meal, showing them where the local shops and stores are, or taking them on outings to local places of interest.

Many of these scholars want to learn more about God and Christianity. It has even been suggested that reading the Bible will help them to understand cultures with a background in Christianity. This gives a wonderful opportunity to share your faith. Most students will enjoy coming along to a Christmas carol concert or to an Easter celebration. Many students – but by no means all – have lost faith in Communism and are looking for something to fill the vacuum. They may welcome an opportunity to study the Bible.

God is working in marvellous ways through Christians reaching out to Chinese scholars. One student said,

> 'I was like the paralysed man beside the pool of Bethesda waiting for the movement of the waters. But then Jesus passed by and put my life together.'

Another scholar's wife said,

> 'I felt the warmth and love of Jesus drawing me to Him from the very start. I saw it in the eyes and on the faces of Christians, and especially in the life of the Christian girl who worked with me in the Chinese restaurant.'

CCSM and other groups can advise and also provide materials to help you in your outreach. Chinese Bibles and other Christian books are available, as well as cassette tapes in Mandarin and Cantonese. There are also Christian lending libraries in various countries distributing Christian books which are specifically suited to mainland Chinese readers.

A year or two ago I was shown a video which outlined the testimonies of three students, each one a foreigner studying in a Western country. One of them was from China. Each told how he or she had gone abroad to study with the purpose of making money – for personal and probably selfish reasons. Each then shared how he or she had been befriended by a Christian. The ways and the means differed, but the heart was still the same. In each case the Christian took the trouble to reach out and show Christ's love to the foreign student, with the result that each of the three came to a personal faith in Jesus Christ. Now they had a new goal in their lives – to serve Jesus. Indeed one of the three (obviously not the Chinese!) went home and hired a football stadium for an evangelistic meeting in which many came to Christ.

The same principle is true of all the areas of service that I have outlined above. Those who have laboured have found that God has blessed in abundance. Again and again the words of Paul have proved true,

> *'Therefore, my dear brothers, stand firm. Let nothing move you. Always give yourselves fully to the work of the Lord, because you know that your labour in the Lord is not in vain.'* (1 Corinthians 15:58)

All that is required is that we respond to the Lord and start serving the peoples of China and other nations – and do not give up. God will reward it. His word guarantees that it will not be in vain.

Faith Without Deeds is Dead

James, inspired by the Holy Spirit to provoke 'armchair' Christians, lays down a real challenge. He writes,

*'What good is it, my brothers, if a man claims to have
faith but has no deeds? Can such faith save him? Suppose a brother or a sister is without clothes and daily
food. If one of you says to him, "Go, I wish you well;
keep warm and well fed," but does nothing about his
physical needs, what good is it? In the same way, faith
by itself, if it is not accompanied by action, is dead. As
the body without the spirit is dead, so faith without
deeds is dead.'* (James 2:14–17, 26, NIV)

A few years ago, whilst I was in Hong Kong and China,
God spoke to me specifically about the need for Christian
literature for China. He urged upon me the need for action.
I became involved in the production of tens of thousands of
books and booklets for China. I knew nothing about printing, and little about many other aspects of that kind of
work. I was not an expert and a committee would not have
chosen me for such a task. But I did want to do the will of
God – for me and for the Chinese.

I had therefore to walk into Hong Kong and ask the Lord
to help me set up a 'conveyor belt' of translators, checkers,
printers and couriers. It has been a joy to see what God has
done specifically through CCSM and DPM in that area. It
has also been a joy to work with other ministries. The fact is
that God did not choose an expert. He chose a 'responder'.
There is then no excuse for any reading these pages. The
issue is not one of expertise or qualifications. It is one of
faith that leads to works.

Angel James was not a China expert or even specifically
called to that nation. He was a minister in a western nation.
But he organised an appeal to raise funds for one million
New Testaments for China through the British and Foreign
Bible Society. The appeal was so successful that twice that
number were sent. A year before he died in 1858, he wrote
and circulated a pamphlet pleading the interests of China
and calling for one hundred new missionaries to that great
land. Though he had no specific 'calling' to China, he did
what you are being asked to do in this chapter. He heard,
he prayed and he acted. This is what he said,

'The conversion of China is, one way or other, the business of every Christian upon earth – and every Christian upon earth **can** do something for it and ought to do what he can. The man who says, "What have I to do with this matter?" is either ignorant, indolent or covetous and is altogether heartless towards the cause of Christ. He that says, "What concern have I in China's conversion?" just asks the question "What fellowship have I with Christ?" We are all too apt to think of what the church can do and ought to do and not what we individually can do and ought to do, and either through modesty, timidity, or avarice, lose ourselves and our individual obligations in the crowd. Do you then ask whose business the conversion of China is? I answer, yours, whosoever you are who may read this page. Yours, I say, as truly as that of any other man on the face of the earth. Here it is, I offer it to you, and in the name of Christ bid you take it. Take it into your hand, your heart, your purse, your closet – you dare not refuse it!'

James' words are tough words. But they are not just words for a previous generation. They ought not to be ignored by our generation with regards to the China of our day.

I have space only to give a short outline of each of the ministries through which we can serve China and its people. Some I have not included – such as going into China as 'ordinary' tourists, seeking to be available for the Lord to use in any way that He might choose. For many of these ministries you will require additonal information. Fuller descriptions are given in my book *Heartcry for China* and in other books listed in Appendix A. Or write to us at any of the CCSM addresses listed in Appendix B. We want to help.

Chapter 20

Experiencing China's Miracle

'He sent a man before them – Joseph, sold as a slave.
They bruised his feet with shackles, his neck was put in
irons, till what he foretold came to pass, till the word of
the Lord proved him true. The king sent and released
him, the ruler of peoples set him free. He made him
master of his household, ruler over all he possessed, to
instruct his princes as he pleased and teach his elders
wisdom.'   (Psalm 105:17–22, NIV)

A few years ago I took two Western pastors to visit the
late Wang Mingdao in Shanghai. Wang Mingdao was a
pastor in Beijing in the 1940s and '50s, overseeing an
independent Christian church. When he refused to join the
government-controlled Three Self Patriotic Church in the
1950s, he faced nation-wide attacks – and, like brother Ye,
imprisonment from 1955 to 1978.

While we were with him, I asked Wang if he had a
message from the Lord for Christians in the West. He
answered immediately,

'Jesus told His disciples that they should not fear, but
should put their faith in Him. Many stumble and fall
away from Christ, but the commonest cause of stum-
bling is the fear of man.'

We knew these words were not just theory; they were the experience of a man of God purified through the furnace of twenty-three years in prison.

When we left Wang's small apartment we were all subdued and silent. There was no need to add to the words that God had spoken to us through that precious and respected elder brother in Christ. We wanted to reflect on all that the Lord was saying to us. If we in the West want to help our brothers and sisters in China, we need first to be humbled before them and long to experience more of their walk with God. We need to admit that they have learnt some vital truths of the Bible that we have not.

Some of the lessons learnt by God's people in China during recent years are also found in the story of Joseph in Genesis. Jacob, on his death bed, sought by prophetic inspiration of the Holy Spirit, to summarise his son Joseph's life,

> *'Joseph is a fruitful vine, a fruitful vine near a spring, whose branches climb over a wall. With bitterness archers attacked him; they shot at him with hostility. But his bow remained steady, his strong arm stayed flexible, because of the Hand of the Mighty One of Jacob, because of the Shepherd, the Rock of Israel, because of your father's God, Who helps you, because of the Almighty, Who blesses you with blessings of the heavens above, blessings of the deep that lies below, blessings of the breast and womb.'*
>
> (Genesis 49:22–25, NIV)

Verse 23 gives us a powerful description of the suffering that so many of the followers of the Lord Jesus in China have had to endure, particularly during the last forty years. It is an accurate description of the Ye's lives. With bitterness and hostility inspired by spiritual and ideological hatred, the Marxist 'archers' have attacked and grieved the people of God in China. Any honest record of the period since some churches refused to become political agents of the new leadership in 1949 will prove that beyond dispute.

Whether we are attacked by the open 'archers' of a hostile ideology or by the secret ambushes of materialism, there are three great lessons that our brothers and sisters in China can teach us in this spiritual warfare. They are contained in verse 22,

> *'Joseph is a fruitful vine, a fruitful vine near a spring, whose branches climb over a wall.'*

Refreshed by Living Water

Firstly, the Christians in China have lived near a spring. That spring is the Lord Jesus. Jesus said,

> *'If anyone is thirsty, let him come to Me and drink. Whoever believes in Me, as the Scripture has said, streams of living water will flow from within him.'*
>
> (John 7:37–38, NIV)

Our brothers and sisters in China have proved again and again that, even in the most arid and thirsty times, this spring of living water will never run dry. Testimonies of people like the Ye's teach us one simple lesson. When they were flagging and tempted to give up, it was the refreshing water that Jesus provides that gave them new strength to go on. It is not these people who are extraordinary, but Jesus. We can take courage from their experiences. Whatever our condition and situation, we too can drink from the same waters and be satisfied.

Our brothers and sisters in China challenge us to walk more closely with Jesus. How often when we are asked how we are, we preface our reply with 'under the circumstances...' The challenge is to be set free from living 'under the circumstances' to living 'under Jesus'. He is the One Who leads us beside still waters, so that we need not thirst.

Part of their 'secret' lies in their commitment to the word of God, the Bible. There is an enviable zeal and hunger for

His Word and for foundational teaching in China today. A recent letter from China to the Far East Broadcasting Company (who broadcast Christian radio programmes into many lands) reads,

> 'I hope that you, at the radio station, are able to send me the Bible I asked for soon. My spiritual life is shallow, and I have little schooling. How can I understand God's Word? If I interpret it wrongly to someone else, my sin will be great. I can only pray that God sends a prophet from Himself ... to teach us the Bible at our church meeting point so that we do not lead others to destruction. Hallelujah. Amen.'

The fervour of that communication shames us, with our shelves groaning under numerous Bible translations – many of which we never use. Our brothers and sisters in China are like those who, when walking through a desert, find a deep and cool oasis spring. May we learn how to drink deeply from that same spring in whatever desert we might find ourselves.

Fruitful in a Harsh Season

The second lesson that Joseph brings to us from Genesis 49:22 is that we should be fruitful,

> *'Joseph is a fruitful vine, a fruitful vine, near a spring.'*

We have already said that the church in China is recognised by many to be the fastest growing in the world, astonishing though that may seem under so much pressure and hostility, and with such great cost in life and liberty. One reason for this is that Chinese Christians believe God put them where they are so that they might bear fruit. They believe firmly in the uniqueness of Christ and of the Gospel that He brought. Out of this conviction has come phenomenal church growth in China. Scores of itinerant evangelists travel around the country, from village to village and town to town, preaching 'illegally' and seeing many turn to Christ. They may face arrest and even occasionally execution. One seventeen-year-old girl had laboured in the most arduous conditions. She was terribly homesick. Weeping before her fellow evangelists she sobbed, 'We felt so lonely, and yet we continued to struggle for every soul.'

Another young girl in China wrote,

'We are a group of village girls who turned to Christ less than a year ago. At night we go out to preach. The love and strength of God helps us. He guides us when we preach. In just a short period of three to four months, we have set up ten more meeting points in the local area. As the Holy Spirit works so effectively, the church has been growing very fast. There are almost 100 people for each meeting point. As the Lord is with us, we have more confidence. We preach at one meeting point every day. Nevertheless, we know we are weak. We have very little biblical knowledge. Please send me a pocket-size Bible with simplified characters.'

This young, untaught Christian girl in China, finding her new faith in Christ so real, immediately began to share it with others – and bore great fruit. Why? Out of the conviction that men and women are lost without Christ and have the right to hear the good news of the Son of God Who loves them and died for them.

News Network International comments,

'Out of such dedication and faith, revival springs. It is easy to forget that the entire Chinese revival was borne out of the most arduous suffering.'

Revival is due, under God, to the selfless sowing of Christians like these. It is due to a conviction that God has ordained us to bear fruit, and therefore, by the power of

the Holy Spirit working within and through us, whatever
our circumstances and situation, we will bear fruit.

Sadly many in the West do not have this conviction. A
worker for a major missionary society commented to me
that even some elders of evangelical churches were unwill-
ing to state that Jesus meant what He said in John 14:6,

> *'I am the way and the truth and the life. No one comes
> to the Father except through Me.'*

Brought up as we are in an environment where any
approach is acceptable except an exclusive one, we are
tempted to water down the plain teaching of Jesus – that
His work on the cross is totally unique and is the only way
by which fallen man may find his relationship with a holy
God restored. We prefer an approach that blurs the edges
and emphasises mutual respect more than divine truth.

The Bishop of Durham in England, David Jenkins, best
known for his denial of the bodily resurrection of Christ,
once publicly attacked the British government's then agri-
culture minister, John Gummer. Gummer, a committed
Christian, was applauding the present Archbishop of
Canterbury for his statement that the empty tomb of Christ
and the resurrection are not mere symbols, but 'glorious
realities'. Jenkins claimed that Gummer's attitude might
split the church! The vast majority of Christians in China
would wonder why Jenkins even bothered to call himself a
Christian, or perhaps would assume that he was co-
operating with the authorities against the church of Jesus
Christ. If Jesus is not the only Saviour, and is not alive
today, then there is little point in risking loss of jobs,
freedom, or even life for Him.

Selwyn Hughes, writing to Christians about right relationships as a mark of maturity, suggested an interesting
and challenging prayer,

> 'O Father, You relate so powerfully to me with other-
> centred energy. Why is it that I use that energy to

maintain my own intactness rather than sharing it with others? Show me how to love as You love, then I shall be mature.'

The substance of the prayer is obvious – that our culture has taught us to take the grace of God and use it for 'personal wholeness', without understanding that self-oriented religion is rarely if ever profitable – to God or to us. Maybe that is a prayer that we need to use frequently and aggressively.

Reaching Over the Bamboo Wall

The third lesson from Genesis 49:22 is to expect God to cause our branches to reach over the walls that hem us in,

> *'Joseph is a fruitful vine, a fruitful vine near a spring, whose branches climb over a wall.'*

Whether our 'walls' are internal and personal (from character, background or disposition) or whether they are external (from society, or workplace or church), we should expect that

> *'with my God I can scale a wall.'*   (Psalm 18:29, NIV)

Samuel Lam, pastor of an unofficial church in Canton, has faced such 'walls' repeatedly. At around midnight on Thursday, February 22nd, 1990, Public Security Bureau officials entered his church. There were still about one hundred believers worshipping there. Lam was ordered to sign an official paper to register with the TSPM. He refused and was arrested. Almost everything in the church was confiscated – precious Bibles and Christian literature, money, videos, television and tape-recording equipment, all used in the Lord's service. Lam was released after twenty-three hours of detention and ordered to cease from all religious activities. The authorities posted a sign on the church door announcing that further meetings were banned. Lam was subsequently interrogated more than ten times. It was even reported that one or more branches of the Chinese judiciary attempted to have him executed.

Lam knows what is at stake. He has already spent twenty years in prison for his faith. His wife died during his captivity. Paying a price for Christ is not new to him, yet he continues to obey the Lord. He refuses to be 'walled in'. His branches reach over those walls. He carries on with his work and resists government pressure to register with the Three-Self Church on the grounds that it is 'a tool to destroy Christianity.' He says,

'If I registered, ours would become a political church and I could not preach the Bible freely.'

He continues,

'We preach the book of Daniel. Daniel obeyed the authorities until they told him not to pray. Like him, we prefer the lion's den ... If a Christian has never suffered, then he cannot understand God's blessings. He is like a child without training. When we suffer, we should never complain or blame others. We should calm down and depend upon God all the more. In twenty years, I did not deny the Lord once. Praise God, not by myself, but the Lord kept my faith.'

With men and women like Samuel Lam in China, hostility to any choice to follow Jesus is very real and open. 'Christ or Caesar' is brought right up to date. But in other countries that is often not so. Malcolm Muggeridge, the British philosopher who turned to Christ late in life after flirting with Communism in Soviet Russia, illustrated this danger graphically through an interesting analogy. He said that it was possible to boil a frog to death by putting it into cold water and then by very slowly increasing the heat of the water. The frog could jump out at any time, but because the change is so gradual it fails to recognise the danger and slowly heats up with the water until it dies. Muggeridge wanted to warn us in the West that we may become so used to a climate of ungodliness that we do not see our world becoming restricted by greater and greater walls. Our right to proclaim Jesus as Lord is being eroded – though we do not even realise the process is taking place.

The Lord Jesus Himself brings that challenge to the church in Ephesus in Revelation 2. Though there were aspects of their life pleasing to the Lord, He had one fierce warning for them,

> *'Yet I hold this against you: you have forsaken your first love. Remember the height from which you have fallen! Repent and do the things you did at first. If you do not repent, I will come to you and remove your lamp stand from its place.'* (Revelation 2:4–5, NIV)

Not all believers who have suffered persecution from hostile regimes have stood under pressure. Some who held leading positions in the church in China have denied their faith in time of trouble. They have walked away from Christ, seeking personal safety at the expense of their own and other people's relationships with the Lord.

One such example comes to mind from Rumania. Pastor Richard Wurmbrandt told of an incident that took place during the dark days of persecution through which his country passed. In one village Christians were rounded up by the authorities to be shot and dumped into a communal grave. As they waited for their unjust execution, the officer in charge of the firing squad invited them to walk away as free men and women – if they would there and then deny their faith in Christ. Immediately the pastor of the church did so and was permitted to walk away a free man. As he walked back to the village a young man came running from the opposite direction. He had sinned so much that he had been excommunicated from the church. 'I have been unable to live for Jesus,' he said, 'I have dishonoured Him by my life. But I can at least die for my faith in Christ.' So pastor and 'sinner' made their own choice for – and against – Jesus. One accepted walls around him from men who hated God. One, at great price, allowed God to grow his branches over those walls.

Extraordinary Feats by Ordinary People

These are but three of the lessons that we may learn from this China story and from many others. We do not deal just with stories written with paper and ink, but with those that have been written in the lives of human beings like ourselves. If any single point is to be stressed, it is simply that these are ordinary human beings, just like us. They point not to themselves for any credit, but rather to their Saviour and their God and to His hidden miracles.

In that, they make a clear statement to us. By God's love and power, ordinary men and women in a dry and barren place can drink from the well that is Christ; they can bear fruit in a hard season; they can break free from walls that surround them to honour their Saviour. Ordinary men and women have done – and still do – extraordinary exploits through the help of their God.

If they can do these things, why not us? Why are so many of us in the churches outside of China parched by lesser droughts, fruitless in more favourable climates, hemmed in by smaller walls? Is it not time for many of us to come before 'the Mighty One of Jacob, the Shepherd, the Rock of Israel', to confess that we are living lesser lives; and to believe and decide that the God of Joseph, the God of the Ye's, can make us *a fruitful vine, a fruitful vine near a spring, whose branches climb over a wall*?

Is it not time that the affluent church outside of China rose up and followed the Master in His love for China? Is it not time to leap over the walls that keep us from hearing her silent cry, praying for her and providing for her nurture and growth? Will not that help us to experience more of China's hidden miracle for ourselves?

Appendix A

Recommended Reading and Viewing on China

Books

Broomhall, A.J., *Hudson Taylor and China's Open Century* (7 vols.). Hodder and Stoughton and Overseas Missionary Fellowship, England

Brother David (1981), *God's Smuggler to China*. Hodder and Stoughton, London

Choy, L.F. (1981), *On Your Mark*. Christian Communications Ltd, Hong Kong

Danyun (1992), *Lilies Amongst Thorns*, Sovereign World, England

Francis, Lesley (1985), *Winds of Change*. Overseas Missionary Fellowship, London

Kauffman, P.E. (1981), *China the Emerging Challenge: A Christian Perspective*. Baker, Grand Rapids, USA

Lambert, Tony (1991), *Resurrection of the Chinese Church*. Hodder and Stoughton and Overseas Missionary Fellowship, England

Lawrence, Carl (1985), *The Church in China: How it Survives and Prospers Under Communism*. Bethany House, Minneapolis

Lyall, L.T. (1985), *God Reigns in China*. Hodder and Stoughton, London

Lyall, L.T. (1985), *New Spring in China*. Zondervan, Grand Rapids, USA

MacInnis, Donald E. (1972), *Religious Policy and Practice in Communist China*. Hodder and Stoughton, London

Morrison, Peter (1984), *Making Friends with Mainland Chinese Students*. Christian Communications Ltd, Hong Kong

Paterson, Ross (1989), *Heartcry for China*. Sovereign World, England

Wallis, Arthur (1985), *China Miracle*. Kingsway Publications, England

Videos

Chinese Church Support Ministries (1992), *China's Best Kept Secrets*. CCSM

Chinese Church Support Ministries (1993), *Heartcry for China*. CCSM

Derek Prince Ministries–China (1992), *China and Mongolia Outreach*. DPM

Appendix B

Ministry Addresses

For further information on the situation in the church and what you can do to help, please write to your local CCSM or DPM office:

CCSM Addresses

Chinese Church Support Ministries
2(b) Carr Lane
Acomb
York YO2 5HU
England

Chinese Church Support Ministries
c/o Malcolm and Barbara Carter
PO Box 1229
Castle Hill
NSW 2154
Australia

Chinese Church Support Ministries
c/o Louisville Covenant Church
232 Carey Avenue
Louisville KY 40218
USA

Chinese Church Support Ministries
PO Box 26–58
Taichung
Taiwan R.O.C.

DPM Addresses

DPM – China
2(b) Carr Lane
Acomb
York YO2 5HU
England

DPM – International
PO Box 300
Fort Lauderdale
FL 33302–0300
USA

DPM – Germany
Internationaler Bibellehrdienst
Markgrafenweg 19
D–72213 Altensteig
Germany

DPM – South Pacific
PO Box 2029
Christchurch
New Zealand

DPM – Australia
Unit 1/14 Pembury Road
Minto
NSW 2566
Australia

DPM – Canada
PO Box 5217
Halifax
Nova Scotia B3L 4S7
Canada

DPM – Asia
PO Box 633
Fanling PO
NT
Hong Kong